Baggett

MICHELIN
Travel Publications

New York City

must
SEES

Chief Editor	Cynthia Clayton Ochterbeck
Senior Editor	M. Linda Lee
Writer	Shea Dean
Production Coordinator	Allison M. Simpson
Cartography	Peter Wrenn
Photo Editor	Brigitta L. House
Documentation	Martha Hunt; Gayle Sparks Miller
Proofreader	Margo Browning
Production	Octavo Design and Production, Inc. Apopka, Florida
Cover Design	Paris Venise Design Paris, 17e
Printing and Binding	Quebecor World Laval, Québec

Michelin North America
One Parkway South
Greenville, SC 29615
USA
800-423-0485
www.michelin-us.com
email: TheGreenGuide@us.michelin.com

Special Sales:

For information regarding bulk sales, customized editions and premium sales, please contact our Customer Service Departments:

USA – 800-423-0485 **Canada** – 800-361-8236

Manufacture française des pneumatiques Michelin
Société en commandite par actions au capital de 304 000 000 EUR
Place des Carmes-Déchaux — 63 Clermont-Ferrand (France)
R.C.S. Clermont-FD B 855 800 507

Note to the reader:

While every effort is made to ensure that all information in this guide is correct and up-to-date, Michelin Travel Publications (Michelin North America, Inc.) accepts no liability for any direct, indirect or consequential losses howsoever caused so far as such can be excluded by law.

Admission prices listed for sights in this guide are for a single adult, unless otherwise specified.

Welcome To New York City

Westin New York at Times Square

Table of Contents

Table of Contents

THE MICHELIN STARS

For more than 75 years, travelers have used the Michelin stars to take the guesswork out of planning a trip. Our star-rating system helps you make the best decision on where to go, what to do, and what to see. A three-star rating means it's one of the "absolutelys"; two stars means it's one of the "should sees"; and one star says it's one of the "sees"—a must if you have the time.

★★★	Absolutely Must See
★★	Really Must See
★	Must See

Three-Star Sights ★★★

American Museum of Natural History ★★★
Bronx Zoo ★★★
Brooklyn Bridge ★★★
Central Park ★★★
Chrysler Building ★★★
The Cloisters ★★★
Empire State Building ★★★
Frick Collection ★★★
Hudson River Valley ★★★
The Metropolitan Museum of Art ★★★
Museum of Modern Art (MoMA) ★★★
Rockefeller Center ★★★
Statue of Liberty ★★★
United Nations Headquarters ★★★
Woolworth Building ★★★

Two-Star Sights ★★

Boscobel Restoration ★★
Broadway ★★
Brooklyn Botanic Garden ★★
Brooklyn Heights ★★
Brooklyn Museum of Art ★★
Cathedral of
St. John the Divine ★★
    Channel Gardens ★★
Chinatown ★★
Citigroup Center ★★
City Hall ★★
Diamond and Jewelry Way ★★
Ellis Island
    Immigration Museum ★★
Forbes Galleries ★★

GE Building ★★
Grand Central
Terminal ★★
Greenwich Village ★★
Guggenheim Museum ★★
The Hamptons ★★
Hispanic Society of
    America ★★
Home of FDR NHS ★★
Isamu Noguchi
    Garden Museum ★★
Jones Beach SP ★★
Kykuit ★★
Lever House ★★
Lincoln Center ★★

Long Island★★
The Long Island Museum★★
Museum of the City
    of New York★★
National Museum of the
    American Indian★★
New York Aquarium★★
New York Botanical Garden★★
New-York Historical Society★★
New York Public Library★★
Old Bethpage
    Village Restoration★★
Pierpont Morgan Library★★
Planting Fields★★
Radio City Music Hall★★

Saint Patrick's Cathedral★★
Seagram Building★★
SoHo★★
Sony Tower★★
South Street Seaport
    Historic District★★
St. Paul's Chapel★★
Times Square★★
Trinity Church★★
Upper East Side★★
Upper West Side★★
Verrazano-Narrows Bridge★★
Villard Houses★★
West Point★★
Whitney Museum
    of American Art★★

One-Star Sights ★

Alice Austen House Museum★
American Museum
    of the Moving Image★
American Numismatic Society★
Asia Society★
Audubon Terrace★
Battery Park★
Brooklyn Academy of Music★
Bryant Park★
Carnegie Hall★
Castle Clinton NM★
CBS Building★
Central Park Wildlife Center★
Chelsea★
Cold Spring Harbor
    Whaling Museum★
Cooper-Hewitt National
    Design Museum★
Daily News Building★
Equitable Center★
Federal Hall NM★
Fire Island★
Fire Island National Seashore★
Flatiron Building★
Fraunces Tavern Museum★
General Grant NM★
Gracie Mansion★
Harlem★
Historic Richmond Town★
International Center of Photography★
Jacques Marchais
    Museum of Tibetan Art★

Jewish Museum★
Little Italy★
Lower East Side
    Tenement Museum★
Madison Avenue★
Metropolitan Life Building★
Morris-Jumel Mansion★
Museum for African Art★
Museum of Arts
    and Design★
Museum of Television
    and Radio★
Neue Galerie★
New York Stock Exchange★
Prospect Park★
Sag Harbor★
    Sagamore Hill NHS★
Staten Island Ferry★
Studio Museum in Harlem★
Sunken Meadow SP★
Theodore Roosevelt
    Birthplace NHS★
TriBeCa★
Trump Tower★
Trump World Tower★
Union Square★
Vanderbilt Museum★
Washington Square★
Wave Hill★
World Trade Center Site★
Yankee Stadium★

*The following abbreviations appear in this list: NHS National
Historic Site; NM National Monument; SP State Park.*

Calendar Of Events

Listed below is a selection of New York City's most popular annual events. Please note that dates may vary from year to year. For more detailed information, contact New York City & Co. *(212-484-1200; www.nycvisit.com).*

January

Chinese New Year Celebrations　212-625-9977
Chinatown　　　www.chinatowninfo.com

Winter Antiques Show　718-292-7392
7th Regiment Armory www.winterantiquesshow.com

February

Westminster Dog Show　212-307-7171
Madison Square Garden
www.westminsterkennelclub.org

March

St. Patrick's Day Parade　212-484-1200
Fifth Ave. from 44th to 86th Sts.
www.saintpatricksdayparade.com

Easter Sunday

Easter Sunday Parade　212-484-1200
Fifth Ave. from 57th St. to Rockefeller Center

April

Cherry Blossom Festival　718-623-7333
Brooklyn Botanic Garden　www.bbg.org

New York International Auto Show　800-282-3336
Jacob K. Javits Center　www.autoshowny.com

May

Fleet Week　212-245-0072
Intrepid Sea-Air-Space Museum
Pier 86　　www.intrepidmuseum.org

Martin Luther King Jr. Parade　212-484-1200
Fifth Ave. from 44th to 86th Sts.

Ninth Avenue International Food Festival 212-581-7029
Ninth Ave., from 37th to 57th Sts.

June

Belmont Stakes　516-488-6000
Belmont Park　www.nyra.com/belmont

JVC Jazz Festival New York　212-501-1390
Various locations　www.festivalproductions.net

Lesbian, Gay, Bisexual and Transgender Pride Week
Various locations
212-807-7433
www.nycpride.org

Mermaid Parade　718-372-5159
Coney Island　www.coneyislandusa.com

Met in the Parks (free concert series)　212-362-6000
Various locations　www.metopera.org

Museum Mile Festival　212-606-2296
Fifth Ave.　www.museummilefestival.org

National Puerto Rican Day Parade   718-401-0404
   Fifth Ave.   www.nationalpuertoricandayparade.org

Shakespeare in the Park   212-539-8750
   Delacorte Theater, Central Park   www.publictheater.org

SummerStage in Central Park   212-360-2777
   Rumsey Playfield   www.summerstage.org

July

Macy's Independence Day Fireworks Celebration
   East River at 34th St.   212-494-4495
   and at South Street Seaport

Mostly Mozart Festival   212-546-2656
   Lincoln Center   www.lincolncenter.org

August

Harlem Week   212-862-8477
   Various locations   www.harlemdiscover.com

Lincoln Center Out of Doors   212-546-2656
   Lincoln Center plazas   www.lincolncenter.org

US Open Tennis Tournament   718-760-6200
   USTA National Tennis Center   www.usta.com
   Flushing, Queens

September

Culture Fest   212-484-1222
   Battery Park   www.nycvisit.com

Feast of San Gennaro   212-768-9320
   Mulberry St., Little Italy   www.littleitalyny.com

New York Film Festival   212-875-5610
   Lincoln Center   www.filmlinc.com/nyff/nyff.htm

October

Columbus Day Parade   212-249-9923
   Fifth Ave. from 44th to 72nd Sts.

Halloween Parade   212-475-3333, ext. 4044
   Greenwich Village

November

Fall Antiques Show   212-777-5218
   7th Regiment Armory, Park Ave. & 67th St.

Macy's Thanksgiving Day Parade   212-494-4495
   77th St. to 34th St.

New York City Marathon   212-860-4455
   Ends in Central Park   www.nyrrc.org

December

Christmas Tree Lighting Ceremony   212-632-3975
   Rockefeller Center

Kwanza Fest   718-585-3530
   Jacob K. Javits Center

Lighting of the Giant Chanukah Menorah   718-778-6000
   Fifth Ave. & 59th St.

New Year's Eve Ball Drop   212-768-1560
   Times Square

Area Codes

Area codes must now be used for every call in New York City.
Dial 1 + area code + seven-digit number.

Manhattan: 212, 646, 917
Bronx, Brooklyn, Queens, Staten Island: 347, 718, 917

PLANNING YOUR TRIP

Before you go, contact New York City's official tourism bureau for information about sightseeing, accommodations, travel packages, recreation opportunities and special events:

NYC & Company

810 Seventh Ave., New York, NY 10019
212-484-1200; www.nycvisit.com

To receive a visitor information packet, call 800-692-8474. Visitor information counselors can be reached at 212-484-1222.

Visitor Centers

Midtown Office – *810 Seventh Ave. between 52nd & 53rd Sts. Take B, D, or E train to 7th Ave. and 53rd St.; N, R, S or Q train to 57th St.; or 1, 9 train to 50th St.*

Downtown Kiosk – Southern tip of City Hall Park on the Broadway sidewalk of Park Row. *Take 1 or 2 train to Park Place; N, R, 4, 5, or 6 train to Brooklyn Bridge/City Hall; A or C train to Broadway/Nassau; or E train to World Trade Center/Chambers St.*

Times Square – In the Embassy Movie Theatre *(1560 Broadway between 46th & 47th Sts.; www.timessquarebid.org)*. This visitor center has brochures, tour information, ATMs, and discount tickets to Broadway and off-Broadway shows. *Take any train to Times Square.*

CityPass – Consider buying a CityPass booklet *($45 adults, $39 children ages 6-17)*, which gives you substantially discounted admissions and allows you to skip lines at the following attractions: American Museum of Natural History, Guggenheim Museum, Museum of Modern Art, Intrepid Sea-Air-Space Museum, Circle Line Harbor Cruise, and Empire State Building Observatory and Skyride. Buy your CityPass online *(http://citypass.net)* or at any of the participating attractions.

Web Sites – *For a list of useful Web sites for New York City, see front cover flap.*

In The News

The city's leading daily newspaper, the *New York Times (www.nytimes.com)*, has comprehensive listings of film, theater, art galleries, museum exhibitions and special events in its two-part Weekend section *(Fri)*, and in the Arts & Leisure section *(Sun)*. Local weeklies, including the *New Yorker, New York Magazine, Time Out New York,* and the *Village Voice*, also have listing sections. They're available at newsstands throughout the city.

TIPS FOR SPECIAL VISITORS

Disabled Travelers – Federal law requires that businesses (including hotels and restaurants) provide access for the disabled, devices for the hearing impaired, and designated parking spaces. For further information, contact the Society for Accessible Travel and Hospitality (SATH), 347 Fifth Ave., Suite 610, New York, NY 10016 *(212-447-7284; www.sath.org)*.

All national parks have facilities for the disabled, and offer free or discounted passes. For details, contact the National Park Service *(Office of Public Inquiries, P.O. Box 37127, Room 1013, Washington, DC 20013-7127; 202-208-4747; www.nps.gov)*.

Passengers who will need assistance with train or bus travel should give advance notice to Amtrak *(800-872-7245 or 800-523-6590/TDD; www.amtrak.com)* or Greyhound *(800-752-4841 or 800-345-3109/TDD; www.greyhound.com)*. Reservations for hand-controlled rental cars should be made in advance with the rental company.

Senior Citizens – Many hotels, attractions and restaurants offer discounts to visitors age 62 or older (proof of age may be required). **The American Association of Retired Persons** (AARP), *(601 E St. NW, Washington, DC 20049; 202-424-3410; www.aarp.com)* offers discounts to its members.

Important Phone Numbers	
Emergency (24hrs)	911
Police (non-emergency, Mon–Fri 9am–6pm)	212-374-5000
Medical Services – House calls USA	800-468-3537
Dental emergencies (24hrs) – NYU College of Dentistry	212-443-1300
Poison Control	212-764-7667
24-hour Pharmacies:	
CVS, 4 locations in Manhattan	800-746-7287
Duane Reade, 224 W. 57th St.	212-541-9708
Rite Aid, 6 locations in Manhattan	800-748-3243
Time	212-976-1616
Weather	212-976-1212

WHEN TO GO

New York has four distinct seasons. Fall, with its crisp, cool days is the debut of the cultural season. The city can be hot and muggy in summer, but it can also feel calmer since many residents leave town during July and August. There are more outdoor events during the summer, including free films, music and theater in city parks. Weather in the brief spring ranges from balmy to rainy to frigid; May is lovely, though, as the city's parks and gardens burst into bloom. Winter normally brings some snow, and holiday decorations and festivities abound.

New York City Average Seasonal Temperatures (recorded at Central Park)				
	Jan	Apr	July	Oct
Avg. High	38°F / 3°C	61°F / 16°C	85°F / 29°C	66°F / 19°C
Avg. Low	26°F / -3°C	44°F / 7°C	70°F / 20°C	50°F / 10°C

Must Know: Practical Information

GETTING THERE

By Air – New York City is served by three airports: two in the borough of Queens and one in New Jersey. They are all run by the Port Authority of New York and New Jersey. In all three airports, ground transportation and information booths are located on the baggage-claim level.

John F. Kennedy International Airport (JFK) – 15mi southeast of Midtown Manhattan *(718-244-4444; www.panynj.gov)*.

LaGuardia Airport (LGA) – 8mi northeast of Midtown Manhattan *(718-533-3400; www.panynj.gov)*.

Newark Liberty International Airport (EWR) – 16mi southwest of Midtown Manhattan *(973-961-6000. www.panynj.gov)*.

By Train – Daily service to New York's **Penn Station** *(32nd St. & Seventh Ave.)* is provided by Amtrak *(800-872-7245; www.amtrak.com)* as well as by the commuter lines of the Long Island Railroad *(718-217-5477)* and New Jersey Transit *(973-762-5100)*. Grand Central Station *(42nd St. & Park Ave.)* is served by Metro-North *(212-532-4900)*, which runs trains from Manhattan to New Haven, Connecticut, and to Poughkeepsie, New York.

By Bus – The **Port Authority Bus Terminal** *(42nd St. & 8th Ave; 212-564-8484)* is the city's main bus terminal and is used by both long-distance and commuter carriers. For schedules, routes and fares for trips throughout the US, contact Greyhound *(800-229-9424; www.greyhound.com)*. For service in the Northeast, contact Peter Pan *(800-343-9999; www.peterpanbus.com)*.

By Car – New York City is situated at the crossroads of **I-95** (north-south) and **I-80** (east-west). Four tunnels and six major bridges lead into Manhattan from all directions; most of them have tolls.

Car Rental Company	Reservations	Web site
Alamo	800-327-9633	www.alamo.com
Avis	800-331-1212	www.avis.com
Budget	800-527-0700	www.drivebudget.com
Dollar	800-800-4000	www.dollar.com
Enterprise	800-325-8007	www.enterprise.com
Hertz	800-654-3131	www.hertz.com
National	800-227-7368	www.nationalcar.com
Thrifty	800-331-4200	www.thrifty.com

GETTING AROUND

By Car – It's best to avoid driving in New York City, but if you must, stay off the roads during rush hours *(weekdays between 7am–9am & 4:30pm–6pm)*. Single-occupancy passenger cars are prohibited from entering Manhattan by any of the midtown or downtown bridges and tunnels weekdays from 6am–10am. Mandatory carpooling is in effect at the Holland Tunnel 24hrs a day. Use of seat belts is required. Child safety seats are mandatory for children under 4 years (seats are available from rental-car agencies). In the state of New York it is illegal to drive with a **mobile phone** in your hand.

By Foot – New York is a very walkable city, but addresses don't indicate the cross streets of a particular location (that is, you can't figure out just from the number where a building is located on the street). Before heading to a site, always find out the cross-street first, so you know how far away it is.

By Public Transportation – The Metropolitan Transportation Authority (MTA) oversees an extensive network of subways, buses and commuter trains throughout the area. Contact MTA's Travel Information Center *(718-330-1234; www.mta.nyc.ny.us/nyct)* for route and fare information.

Subway – *For subway map and information, see inside back cover.*

City Buses – New York City Transit buses generally operate daily 5:30am–2am. Buses on some major routes run 24hrs/day. Route maps are posted at bus stops and on buses. Rides *($2)* can be deducted from a MetroCard or paid in exact change.

Taxis – *www.nyc.gov/html/tlc*. Only yellow taxi cabs with roof medallions showing the taxi number are autho-rized to pick up passengers on the street (numbers are illuminated on empty taxis). Rate schedule: $2 for the first 1/5mi, 30¢ for each addi-tional 1/5mi, and 20¢ per minute of waiting time.

> **The Grid**
>
> Manhattan's streets are laid out in a grid pattern (exceptions are Greenwich Village and the Financial District). Streets run east-west and avenues run north-south. Fifth Avenue is the dividing line between east and west addresses. Downtown is south; uptown, north. "Downtown" also refers to the area below 14th Street. Midtown stretches roughly from 34th Street to 59th Street; Uptown is the area north of that. The majority of streets in Manhattan are one-way.

FOREIGN VISITORS

Visitors from outside the US can obtain information from the multilingual staff at NYC & Co. or from the US embassy or consulate in their country of residence (many foreign countries also maintain consulates in New York City). For a com-plete list of American consulates and embassies abroad, visit the US State Department Bureau of Consular Affairs listing on the Internet at: *http://travel.state.gov/links.html*.

Entry Requirements – Starting October 1, 2003, travelers entering the United States under the Visa Waiver Program (VWP) must have a machine-readable passport. Any traveler without a machine-readable passport will be required to obtain a visa before entering the US. Citizens of VWP countries are permitted to enter the US for general business or tourist purposes for a maximum of 90 days without needing a visa. Visa Waiver Program requirements can be found on the official Visa Services Web site *(http://travel.state.gov/vwp.html)*.

Must Know: Practical Information

All citizens of nonparticipating countries must have a visitor's visa. Upon entry, nonresident foreign visitors must present a valid passport and round-trip transportation ticket. Canadian citizens are not required to present a passport or visa, but they must present a valid picture ID and proof of citizenship. Naturalized Canadian citizens should carry their citizenship papers.

US Customs – All articles brought into the US must be declared at the time of entry. Prohibited items: plant material; firearms and ammunition (if not for sporting purposes); meat or poultry products. For information, contact the US Customs Service at 1300 Pennsylvania Ave. NW, Washington, DC 20229 *(202-354-1000; www.customs.gov/travel/travel.htm)*.

Money and Currency Exchange – Visitors can exchange currency at downtown banks as well as in the International Terminal of all three airports. Banks, stores, restaurants and hotels accept travelers' checks with picture identification. To report a lost or stolen credit card: American Express *(800-528-4800)*; Diners Club *(800-234-6377)*; MasterCard *(800-307-7309)*; or Visa *(800-336-8472)*.

Driving in the US – Visitors bearing valid driver's licenses issued by their country of residence are not required to obtain an International Driver's License. Drivers must carry vehicle registration and/or rental contract, and proof of automobile insurance at all times. Gasoline is sold by the gallon. Vehicles in the US are driven on the right-hand side of the road.

Electricity – Voltage in the US is 120 volts AC, 60 Hz. Foreign-made appliances may need AC adapters (available at specialty travel and electronics stores) and North American flat-blade plugs.

Taxes and Tipping – Prices displayed in the US do not include sales tax (8.6% in New York City), which is not reimbursable. It is customary to give a small gift of money—a **tip**—for services rendered to waiters (15-20% of bill), porters ($1 per bag), chamber maids ($1 per day) and cab drivers (15% of fare).

Measurement Equivalents

Degrees Fahrenheit	95°	86°	77°	68°	59°	50°	41°	32°	23°	14°
Degrees Celsius	35°	30°	25°	20°	15°	10°	5°	0°	-5°	-10°

1 inch = 2.54 centimeters   1 foot = 30.48 centimeters
1 mile = 1.609 kilometers   1 pound = 0.454 kilograms
1 quart = 0.946 liters   1 gallon = 3.785 liters

ACCOMMODATIONS
For a list of suggested accommodations, see Must Stay.

Reservations Services:
Central Reservation Services – 800-555-7555; www.reservation-services.com.
City Hotel Finder – 888-649-6331; www.cityhotelfinder.com.
Express Hotel Reservations – 800-407-3351; www.express-res.com.
City Lights Bed and Breakfast – 212-737-7049.
The Inn Keeper – 941-484-1952; www.theinnkeeper.com.
Manhattan Getaways – 212-956-2010; www.manhattangetaways.com.
New World Bed and Breakfast – 212-675-5600.

Hostels – *www.hostels.com*. A no-frills, inexpensive alternative to hotels, hostels are a great choice for budget travelers. Prices average $25–$75 per night.

Major hotel and motel chains with locations in New York City include:

Property	Phone/Web site	Property	Phone/Web site
Best Western	800-528-1234 www.bestwestern.com	Hyatt	800-233-1234 www.hyatt.com
Comfort, Clarion & Quality Inns	800-228-5150 www.comfortinn.com	ITT Sheraton	800-325-3535 www.sheraton.com
Fairmont	877-441-1414 www.fourseasons.com	Marriott	800-228-9290 www.marriott.com
Four Seasons	212-758-5700 www.fourseasons.com	Radisson	800-333-3333 www.radisson.com
Helmsley	212-888-1624 www.helmsleyhotles.com	Ritz-Carlton	800-241-3333 www.ritzcarlton.com
Hilton	800-445-8667 www.hilton.com	W Hotels	888-848-5144 www.starwood.com
Holiday Inn	800-465-4329 www.holiday-inn.com	Westin	800-848-0016 www.westin.com
Howard Johnson	800-446-4656 www.hojo.com		

SPORTS

New York City is a great place to be a spectator where sports are concerned. The city's major professional sports teams include:

Sport/Team	Season	Venue	info #/tickets #	Web site
Baseball/New York Mets (National League)	Apr-Oct	Shea Stadium	718-507-6387 718-507-8499	http://newyork.mets.mlb.com
Baseball/New York Yankees (AL)	Apr-Oct	Yankee Stadium	718-293-4300 212-307-1212	http://newyork.yankees.mlb.com
Football/New York Giants (NFC)	Sept-Dec	Giants Stadium	201-935-8111 201-935-8222	www.giants.com
Football/New York Jets (AFC)	Sept-Dec	Giants Stadium	tickets & info: 516-560-8200	www.newyorkjets.com
Men's Basketball/New York Knicks (NBA)	Oct-Apr	Madison Square Garden	212-465-5867 212-307-7171	www.nba.com/knicks/
Women's Basketball/New York Liberty (WNBA)	May-Aug	Madison Square Garden	212-564-9622 877-962-2849	www.wnba.com/liberty/
Hockey/New York Rangers (NHL)	Oct-Apr	Madison Square Garden	212-465-6000 212-307-7171	www.newyorkrangers.com
Soccer/New York/New Jersey MetroStars (MLS)	Mar-Oct	Giants Stadium	201-583-7000 212-307-7171	www.metrostars.com

New York City

All That Glitters: New York City

The City That Never Sleeps. The Big Apple. No matter what you call it, New York packs a staggering world into about 320 square miles. With some eight million residents at last count, New York is by far the most populous city in the US. It's a global melting pot, a cultural magnet, an economic powerhouse. It's not for nothing that New Yorkers have a reputation for being swaggering and brash. Theirs is one great city.

It's also a relatively young one. European settlement began in earnest here in 1625, when the Dutch East India Company established the Nieuw Amsterdam trading post at the southern tip of Manhattan Island. That name, which comes from an Algonquian term meaning "island of hills," suggests that the natives ventured farther than the colonists, who for the better part of 200 years remained on flat land near the shore, behind a defensive wall (today's Wall Street).

The transfer of authority from Dutch to British hands in 1664—and the new name, after the Duke of York—didn't phase early New Yorkers, most of whom had little allegiance to either crown. They were here to make money.

Manhattan, as it turns out, was perfectly suited to global trade, thanks to the snug arrangement of other land masses around its harbor. As port activity grew, so

Fast Facts

- With an area of 22.7sq mi, Manhattan is the smallest of the city's five boroughs. It is also the most densely populated county in the US, with 1.5 million residents.

- In 2000, 36 percent of New Yorkers were foreign-born, up from 25 percent in 1980.

- New York's $400 billion economy would rank 15th among the nations of the world.

- The New York Yankees have won 26 World Series, more than any other team in baseball.

- The average speed of a car traveling in traffic-clogged Manhattan during the day is 7mph.

did friction with the British system of "taxation without representation." When war broke out, the British took over the city almost immediately and occupied it until independence.

After briefly serving as US capital, New York established the financial institutions that led the new nation into the Industrial Age. In 1792 brokers met under a buttonwood tree at Wall and Williams streets and founded the forerunner to the New York Stock Exchange. Around the turn of the 19C Manhattan's gridiron plan was laid out, and the exploding population spread northward.

After the 363mi Erie Canal linked the city with the Great Lakes in 1825, New York became the nation's preeminent port and shipbuilding capital. The city's leading businessmen leveraged this advantage skillfully, investing their profits in new building projects. New York's population doubled every 20 years, fed by waves of European immigrants, who would help build the city not just with their hands but with their ideas.

The dynamism and density of New York City pushed the decision to build farther into the sky than had ever been done before. In the second half of the 20C the city solidified its international position in industry, commerce and finance, and its skyline, newly bristling with skyscrapers, reflected that prosperity.

New York's growth has not been without setbacks. A cholera epidemic in 1832 killed 4,000 citizens. A fire in 1845 leveled 300 buildings. In 1975 the city defaulted into bankruptcy. And the September 11, 2001, terrorist attack took 2,800 lives as well as one of the city's proudest landmarks, the World Trade Center. But New York City has proved remarkably resilient to such tragedies. Ambitious plans to rebuild downtown Manhattan into a model 21C city are well on their way to fruition. These plans have their critics, but in New York, that's all part of the process. The results speak for themselves.

Looking around you in New York isn't enough: you have to look *up* to notice some of the city's finest features. From the Woolworth Building's copper crown to Sony Tower's "Chippendale" roofline, some surprises lurk up there in the clouds. Here's a key to some of them; for the full scoop on New York's changing skyline, visit the new **Skyscraper Museum**, which opened in fall 2003 in Battery Park City *(212-968-1961; www.skyscraper.org)*.

Chrysler Building★★★

405 Lexington Ave. at 42nd St. 4,5,6 or 7 train to Grand Central.

When you have money, you can do anything. Or so Walter P. Chrysler must have thought when he commissioned architect William Van Alen to design the world's tallest building. One of the first large buildings to use metal exten-

sively on its exterior, the 77-story Art Deco landmark pays sparkling homage to the car. It was briefly the world's tallest building in 1930, after its architect secretly ordered a 185ft spire attached to its crown, edging out the Bank of Manhattan, which was 2ft taller. Alas, the distinction lasted only a few months; the Empire State Building blew both buildings away when it opened in 1931. Stylistically the Chrysler Building has stood the test of time, though: the six semi-circular arches of its stainless-steel pinnacle, patterned after a 1930 Chrysler radiator cap, glimmer majestically during the day and are dramatically lit at night.

An Art Deco masterpiece faced in red African marble, onyx and amber, the **lobby** sports a ceiling mural by Edward Trumbell and ornate elevator doors decorated with inlaid woods.

They Don't Call It The Chrysler Building For Nothing

Developed by automobile magnate Walter P. Chrysler, the building that shares his name incorporates abundant automotive decorations in its various setbacks. Crane your neck and see if you can spot the following elements:

- Aluminum trim
- Gargoyles in the form of radiator caps
- Stylized racing cars
- Metal hubcaps
- Car fenders
- Silver hood ornaments

Woolworth Building★★★

223 Broadway at Barclay St. Any train to City Hall.

New York's "Cathedral of Commerce" was financed by F.W. Woolworth, an Upstate New York native who made his fortune with a nationwide chain of five-and-dime stores. The tallest building in the world from 1913 until 1929, this was architect Cass Gilbert's Gothic masterpiece and New York's first skyscraper. Woolworth paid $13.5 million in cash for his Gotham headquarters, and Gilbert (who also designed the Supreme Court building in the nation's capital) delivered a beauty. The terra-cotta facade (recently replaced with cast stone) shoots upward 30 stories without setbacks, then gives way to a 30-story tower ornamented with gargoyles, pinnacles, flying buttresses and finials. The top is crowned by a copper pyramidal roof.

On its opening day in April 1913, President Woodrow Wilson pressed a button in Washington, DC, turning on 80,000 interior bulbs and exterior floodlights to the oohs and ahs of thousands of spectators.

Lobby★★ – This spectacular space rises three stories to a stained-glass barrel-vaulted ceiling and is decorated with Byzantine-style mosaics and frescoes. Look under the supporting crossbeams on the Barclay Street side for the six caricature bas-reliefs. Among them you'll see Woolworth counting his nickels and architect Gilbert clutching a model of the building.

Citigroup Center★★

153 E. 53rd St. at Lexington Ave. E or V train to Lexington Ave.

You can't miss this 59-story aluminum and glass tower—its crown is set at a 45-degree angle, a standout among the flat roofs of other Midtown skyscrapers. Citigroup Center is home to the parent company of Citibank. Designed by Hugh Stubbins & Associates and completed in 1979, the structure ranks as one of the tallest buildings in the world. Its base is also a wonder: Cut away at the four corners, it stands on a cross-shaped footing. Four colossal pillars, each nine stories (115ft high) tall and 22ft square, are set in the center of each side, rather than at the corners of the building.

St. Peter's Church★ *(below)* and the popular seven-story **Market** nestle beneath the cantilevered corners. A lively complex of shops and restaurants, the Market surrounds a landscaped atrium that is often the scene of exhibits and concerts.

Citicorp Center Construction Facts

• The building's slanted 160ft-tall crown was intended to hold solar panels.

• A computer-operated load mass damper keeps the building stable.

• Double-decker elevator cars leave more space available for offices.

• There was supposed to be residential space on the tower's upper floors, but zoning restrictions nixed that plan.

St. Peter's Church

Access on 54th St. 212-935-2200. www.saintpeters.org. Open year-round daily 9am—9pm. Closed holidays. This Lutheran church sold its land to Citicorp with the understanding that a new church would be integrated within the complex. The result is a comparatively tiny structure whose rooflines repeat the angle of the tower above. Soundproofing makes this place an oasis of silence in an otherwise noisy corner of Midtown. The adjoining Erol Beker Chapel of the Good Shepherd★ was sculpted by Louise Nevelson as a "place of purity" in Manhattan.

GE Building ★★

30 Rockefeller Plaza. B, D, F or V train to 47th-50th Sts./Rockefeller Center.

This lithe 70-story skyscraper (originally the RCA Building) is Rockefeller Center's tallest and finest structure. It was finished in 1933, and John D. moved the Rockefeller family offices into the building shortly thereafter. Its strong vertical lines, softened with staggered setbacks in the upper stories, are considered a triumph of Art Deco design. To see them without breaking your neck, go to the Channel Gardens on the other side of the skating rink and look up, up, up.

Lobby – The murals by Spanish artist Jose Maria Sert are actually the second set to adorn these walls. The first, by the Mexican artist Diego Rivera, were destroyed for their anti-capitalist themes. Rivera re-created them in Mexico City, adding a likeness of John D. Rockefeller drinking a martini with a few "painted ladies."

Rainbow Room★ – You'll get some of the best views in the city from this 65th-floor institution, where world-class cabaret acts perform nightly *(see Musts for Fun)*.

NBC Studios – The National Broadcasting Company shoots *NBC Nightly News,* the sketch-comedy classic *Saturday Night Live,* and other shows in studios here.

NBC Studio Tour

Ever wonder what goes on inside that little glowing box you call a TV? Here's your chance to find out. One-hour tours lead guests through the network's "golden days" in radio, in and around several studio sets, and past the high-tech equipment used to film sporting events. *For information, call 212-664-4000 or log on to www.nbc.com.*

Flatiron Building ★

175 5th Ave. at 23rd St. N or R train to 23rd St.

Even if you've never been to New York City, you've likely seen this building before—it's a popular prop on television shows and movies. When you see it from the north side, the striking triangular structure looks like an iron, though some New Yorkers have compared it to the prow of a ship (think cruise ship) for its unbroken facade. Though it's only 6ft wide at its sharp corner, the Flatiron Building rises 22 stories straight up from the sidewalk.

Famed Chicago architect Daniel H. Burnham came up with the building's triangular shape as a clever solution to the problem of the awkward building site he was faced with at the corner of Broadway and Fifth Avenue. Completed in 1902, the Flatiron Building ushered in the age of the skyscraper with its steel framework, which Burnham pioneered in this project. Like many of his other works, the Flatiron Building (anchor of the Flatiron District) is made to look old with its limestone and terra-cotta exterior. The enormous cornice that tops the building makes its looming presence above the street even more pronounced.

Always A Great Notion

Daniel Burnham had the right idea when he said: "Make no little plans; they have no magic to stir men's blood."

The Rest of the Best: More Skyscrapers

Bold letters in brackets refer to map on the inside front cover.

Lever House ★ ★ [A] – *390 Park Ave.* Designed by Skidmore, Owings, and Merrill in 1952, this elegant 21-story vertical slab of blue-green glass and stainless steel sparked the building boom that replaced Park Avenue's sedate stone apartment buildings with "glass box" corporate headquarters.

Seagram Building ★ ★ [B] – *375 Park Ave.* The 38-story Seagram Building, designed in 1958 by Mies van der Rohe and Philip Johnson, is considered one of the finest International-style skyscrapers in New York and served as a model for office towers worldwide.

Sony Tower ★ ★ (former AT&T Headquarters) **[C]** – *550 Madison Ave. at 55th St.* New Yorkers call it the "Chippendale building" for its roofline, which looks like the top of a Colonial armoire; architecture buffs have dubbed it the first post-Modern skyscraper (1984, Philip Johnson and John Burgee).

CBS Building ★ [D] – *51 W. 52nd St. at Sixth Ave.* Known as the Black Rock, the 38-story CBS Building is the only high-rise building designed by Finnish-born architect Eero Saarinen.

Daily News Building★ – *220 E. 42nd St., between Second & Third Aves.* Vertical "stripes," (white brick piers alternating with patterned red and black brick spandrels) make the 1930 Daily News Building look taller than its 37 stories. The lobby is famed for its huge revolving globe—12ft in diameter—and the clock that gives readings in 17 time zones.

Equitable Center★ **[E]** – *Seventh Ave., between 51st & 52nd Sts.* The block-long complex named for the insurance company features as its centerpiece Equitable Tower (1985), a 54-story granite, limestone and glass structure designed by Edward Larrabee Barnes.

Metropolitan Life Building★ – *1 Madison Ave. at 24th St.* This square Renaissance Revival tower (1909, Le Brun and Sons), which looks like a brightly lit castle at night, is known for its gargantuan four-sided clock, whose hour hands weigh 700 pounds apiece.

Trump Tower★ **[F]** – *725 Fifth Ave. at 56th St.* Rising 58 stories, this dark glass-sheathed tower has myriad tiny setbacks, many topped with trees and shrubs, giving the appearance of a hanging garden. Its six-story, pink-marble atrium contains a high-end shopping center with an 80ft waterfall.

The World Bar

Sophistication and understatement reign at the World Bar, in the Trump World Tower's lobby. As if to foster after-hours diplomacy for its neighbor the United Nations, the music is kept low, the banquettes private, the service discreet. The only thing not understated here is Trump's signature drink, the World's Most Expensive Cocktail, a $50 amalgam of cognac, champagne and, yes, potable gold.

Trump World Tower★ – *First Ave. & 48th St.* Looming over the U.N. complex, Donald Trump's 2001 contribution to the New York skyline is a slender, 72-story bronze-colored glass box, the tallest residential building in the world.

S tatue of Liberty, Empire State Building, Brooklyn Bridge. Your little-town blues will melt away when you see these awesome icons of The Big Apple. Some of these buildings are lucky to still be here. For years New Yorkers thought city land was too valuable for buildings to be "marked." That attitude changed after Pennsylvania Station was demolished in 1965, and the Landmarks Preservations Commission was formed as a result.

Brooklyn Bridge★★★

Adjacent to South Street Seaport, the bridge connects Downtown with Brooklyn. N or R train to City Hall.

Psst, wanna buy a bridge? With its great Gothic towers and its spider's web of cables, the Brooklyn Bridge is one of New York's best-known landmarks. Building it wasn't easy. German-born John Augustus Roebling got the commission to design it in 1869, but shortly after the plans were approved, one of his feet was crushed while he was taking measurements for the piers. Despite an amputation, gangrene set in and he died three weeks later. His son Washington Roebling took over the project, but he was injured too, getting the bends in an underwater expedition to build the foundations. Washington oversaw construction from his sickbed from that point on.

Finally, after 14 years of work, the link between Brooklyn and Manhattan was made in 1883. And with what style—New York had a world-class monument at last! It ranked as the largest bridge in the world until 1903.

Hoofing it – A stroll across the Brooklyn Bridge is one of the most dramatic walks in the city, offering stupendous views, especially at sunset. The pedestrian walkway begins near the Brooklyn Bridge-City Hall subway station in Manhattan, and near the High Street-Brooklyn Bridge station in Brooklyn. Allow about 30 minutes to cross the expanse.

How the Brooklyn Bridge Measures Up

- **Height** – Its towers rise 276ft; the maximum clearance above the water is 133ft.
- **Length** – The bridge stretches 5,989ft, with a center span of 1,595ft between its two towers.
- **Strength** – Four huge cables, interlaced with a vast network of wire, support the steel span. Each 16-inch-thick cable comprises 5,434 separate strands and is 3,515ft long.

Empire State Building★★★

Fifth Ave. & 34th St. 212-736-3100. www.esbnyc.com. Open year-round daily 9:30am–midnight, reduced hours Jan 1 & Dec 24–25. $11. Any train to 34th St.

You probably picture this 102-story Art Deco skyscraper with King Kong climbing its length with a doll-like hysterical Fay Wray in his hand. This famous image is burned into the minds of many, thanks to the 1933 film *King Kong*.

Even so, the Empire State Building is the quintessential New York landmark. Because of its massive footprint and its tapered upper stories, the building seems to play hide-and-seek. You can be standing right next to the Empire State Building and not know it's there, but twenty blocks, or even several miles away it totally dominates the skyline—especially at night, when its crown is lit.

Although construction started just weeks before the stock market crash of 1929, it wasn't slowed by the Depression; in fact, the building sometimes rose more than a story each day. In 1945 a B-25 bomber crashed into the 79th floor, killing the crew and 14 people inside. But the robust structure was undamaged. Today the Empire State Building, including its three-story-high European marble lobby decked out with sleek Art Deco detailing and 73 elevator cars, appears much as it did when it was built.

How Does This Strike You?

A 22-story television antenna, attached to the top of the Empire State Building in 1985, serves as a lightning rod, protecting surrounding buildings by absorbing about 100 lightning strikes a year.

View From The Top

On clear days the view from the open-air, 86th-floor **observatory** is the best in the city, sometimes extending 80mi in all directions.

All visitors to the Empire State Building must enter through the Fifth Avenue entrance. Security is airport-tight, so expect a wait. Take the elevator or escalator to the concourse level to buy observatory tickets *(consult the visibility chart first)*; you can also buy tickets online *(www.esbnyc.com)*. The observatory is open daily from 9:30am to midnight. The last elevator goes up at 11:15pm.

Landmarks

Rockefeller Center★★★

In Midtown, between Fifth & Seventh Aves., and 47th & 52nd Sts. B, D, F, Q or V train to 47th-50th Sts./Sixth Ave.

A "city within a city," the coordinated urban complex of limestone buildings and gardens goes together like a sweater set from Saks Fifth Avenue, with all the proper accessories. Rockefeller Center didn't come into the world so cool and collected; in fact it was born of John D. Rockefeller's desperation to make good on an investment that looked for years like a money pit for the family oil fortune. In 1928 Rockefeller signed a 24-year lease with Columbia University for the core 12 acres. He had grand plans for a colossal new venue to house the Metropolitan Opera, but after the October 1929 stock market crash, the Met pulled out and Columbia wouldn't budge on the terms of the rent. Rockefeller would pay that bill and shell out even more in the next 10 years to demolish 228 smaller buildings and put the initial cluster of 14 Art Deco structures in their place. An elegant ensemble of buildings—there are now 19 on 22 acres— Rock Center combines high and low structures with gardens, public art and underground concourses lined with restaurants.

GE Building★★ – *30 Rockefeller Plaza. See Skyscrapers.*

Radio City Music Hall★★ – *1270 Sixth Ave. See Performing Arts.*

Channel Gardens★★ – *Fifth Ave., between 49th & 50th Sts.* The center's most relaxing public space, with its benches and seasonal flower beds, circles six rectangular pools.

Rockefeller Plaza – This bustling pedestrian concourse slices north-south through the middle of the complex. In winter it hosts a 10-story-tall Christmas tree and, in the lower plaza, a skating rink. In summer the rink gives way to a cafe.

A Piece of the Rock

If you visit Rockefeller Center between 7am and 9am weekdays, you can join the mob of placard-holding tourists who form the human backdrop of the *Today Show*, filmed at NBC's street-level studios *(Rockefeller Plaza & 49th St.)*. Or better yet, you can enjoy a coffee across the plaza at Dean & Deluca and ponder Americans' zeal to be on TV, no matter how silly they look.

Atlas – Fronting the 41-story International Building, the monumental sculpture of the globe-toting god created by Lee Lawrie was picketed at its unveiling for resembling Italian dictator Benito Mussolini.

Statue of Liberty★★★

Liberty Island. 212-363-3200. www.nps.gov/stli. Only the grounds are currently open, daily 9:30am–5pm. Closed Dec 25. For information on visiting, see sidebar below.

Lowdown On Lady Liberty

As of summer 2003, only the grounds of the Statue of Liberty were open to visitors following the September 11, 2001 attacks; call or consult the Web site for updates. You can only reach the island via a ferry that departs from Battery Park *(every 40min)*, on the southern tip of Manhattan, and loops back to pick up and deposit passengers *(at no extra charge)* at Ellis Island. Ferries run from 9:30am to 5pm, with extended hours and more frequent runs in July and August *(212-269-5755; www.statueoflibertyferry.com)*. Another ferry departs from Liberty State Park in New Jersey *(201-435-9499; www.libertystatepark.com)*.

America has France to thank for the statue that guards New York Harbor. With a torch in her hand and broken shackles at her feet, the Statue of Liberty has been welcoming "huddled masses" to New York for more than a century. In 1865 a French historian first thought of memorializing the quest for freedom shared by France and the US. Alsatian sculptor Frédéric-Auguste Bartholdi was sent to America in 1871 to explore the idea.

As Bartholdi watched the city spread out before his approaching ship, he decided that one of the tiny harbor islands would be an ideal site for a figure of Liberty. A joint commission was formed, with the French agreeing to finance the statue and the US committing to pay for the pedestal. In 1874 Bartholdi began work on Liberty, first sculpting clay models and then, for the real thing, applying 300 molded-copper sheets to the 151ft-tall iron and steel skeleton made by French engineer Gustave Eiffel (who would later create the Eiffel tower). The statue was completed in 1884, then dismantled and packed into 220 shipping crates for her transatlantic voyage. Nearly a year passed before the Americans raised enough money for the pedestal, designed by Richard Morris Hunt. The entire package was unveiled on October 28, 1886, with President Grover Cleveland presiding over the foggy ceremony.

Ellis Island Immigration Museum★★ – *See Museums.*

Inside the Pedestal – Dominating the lobby is one of Liberty's previous torches (from 1916). On the second floor is the badly corroded original (the current one dates from 1986) as well as Bartholdi's working models and a collection of Liberty souvenirs. At the top of the pedestal is an observation deck, with views in all directions.

Climb to the Crown – The 354-step (22-story) climb up the winding metal staircase to the crown is not for the claustrophobic. You can see the harbor through the openings in the crown, whose seven points represent the seven continents and the seven seas.

United Nations Headquarters★★★

First Ave., between 42nd & 48th Sts. 212-963-8687. www.un.org. 4, 5, 6 or 7 train to Grand Central. For tour information, see sidebar. Closed on major US and international holidays.

The heady mission of the group who works in this complex of buildings and parks is to "preserve international peace and security, promote self-determination and equal rights, and encourage economic and social well being."

The term "United Nations" was coined by Franklin Delano Roosevelt in 1941 to describe the countries allied against the Axis powers in World War II. Afterward, world leaders saw a need for a permanent peacekeeping force. The U.N. came into being in San Francisco on October 24, 1945, when a majority of its 51 founding members ratified its charter. John D. Rockefeller Jr. lured the group to New York with an $8.5 million gift, which was used to buy 18 acres on the East River. A team of 14 designers from around the world collaborated on the design of the complex, whose overall concept is credited to the French architect Le Corbusier, appropriately a pioneer of the International style. Since its founding the U.N. has grown to incorporate 191 countries.

General Assembly Building – Outside this long, low concrete structure that forms the heart of the U.N., member states' flags are arranged alphabetically from Afghanistan to Zimbabwe, just as their delegations are seated in the assembly hall. In the lobby is a dramatic 15ft-by-20ft stained-glass window by French artist Marc Chagall.

Visiting the U.N.

Visitors enter at 46th St. & First Ave. U.N. buildings can be visited by one-hour guided tour only *(Mon–Fri, 9:30am–4:45pm; Sat–Sun, 10am–4:30pm; $10; children under 5 are not permitted)*. You can buy tickets in the General Assembly building, but be sure to plan ahead; lines are often long due to extensive security checks. Call ahead for schedule and for foreign-language tour availability. There are no parking facilities, so use public transportation.

Secretariat Building – Most distinctive in the complex, this shimmering green-glass slab (1950), which measures 544ft tall (39 stories) but only 72ft wide, houses offices for 7,400 employees. It's not open to the public.

Conference Building – The five-story Conference Building contains meeting space for the U.N.'s three councils.

Landmarks

Grand Central Terminal★★

Park Ave. & 42nd St. www.grandcentralterminal.com. 4, 5, 6 or 7 train to Grand Central.

There's a reason that Grand Central Terminal is held up as the epitome of hustle and bustle (i.e., "It's like Grand Central station around here!"). This magical public space shuffles 500,000 commuters to and from the city each workday. Railroad baron "Commodore" Cornelius Vanderbilt financed its $80 million construction by, quite literally, covering his tracks. In 1903 the city had banned steam locomotives to reduce air and noise pollution, and Vanderbilt had to either go electric or leave the city. He not only electrified his trains but, with the help of engineer William J. Wingus, routed them underground, freeing up a vast stretch of Park Avenue *(between 42nd & 59th Sts.)* for real estate development. He used some of those profits to pay for the Beaux-Arts station. When it opened in 1913, Grand Central Terminal was called "the gateway to the nation," but like many landmarks in New York, it was threatened with demolition in the 1970s. Thanks to the intervention of civic boosters like Jacqueline Kennedy Onassis, it was saved, and a $200 million restoration in the mid-1990s brought it back to its original splendor.

Facade – The 42nd Street facade, of Stony Creek granite and Bedford limestone, has three grand arches flanked by Doric columns. On top is a 13ft clock and Jules-Felix Coutain's 1914 sculpture depicting Mercury, supported by Minerva and Hercules. Below, looking quite tiny on the balcony, stands a bronze statue of Cornelius Vanderbuilt.

Main Concourse – The vaulted turquoise ceiling, decorated with the constellations of the Zodiac (which, oddly, were applied backward by Paul Heleu in 1913), soars to a wondrous height of 12 stories. The marble stairs on the west end were modeled after the grand staircase at the Paris Opera.

> ### Isn't It Grand?
> The Municipal Arts Society leads a free tour of the station Wednesday at 12:30pm. Meet at the information booth on the Grand Concourse *(for information, call 212-935-3960).* Friday at 12:30pm a free tour is led by the Grand Central Partnership. Meet on 42nd Street in front of the Phillip Morris/ Whitney Museum across the street from Grand Central *(for details, call 212-697-1245).*

New York Public Library★★

476 Fifth Ave., between 40th & 42nd Sts. 212-340-0833. www.nypl.org. Open Mon, Wed & Thu 9am–9pm, Tue 11am–7pm, Fri & Sat 10am–6pm. Closed Sun & major holidays. 7 train to 5th Ave.; B, D, F, Q or V train to 42nd St.

To escape the hubbub of Midtown on a warm day, there's nothing like sipping an iced coffee on the New York Public Library's well-worn steps. But you have to go inside to really appreciate what the library has to offer—eclectic, top-notch exhibits and lavish interiors that you can explore free of charge. Here you'll also find a working, if old-fashioned, model of the City Beautiful movement, complete with pneumatic tubes (used by librarians to send requests for books stored in the vaults beneath).

Carrère and Hastings designed the 1911 Beaux-Arts masterpiece. Its imposing Fifth Avenue entrance, made of white Vermont marble, is guarded by two photogenic lions (sculpted by Edward Clark Potter), and its Sixth Avenue backyard is none other than Bryant Park. Eleven thousand visitors from around the globe—no ID required—enter the library daily to admire its architectural treasures and to pore over its 34 million books, which make NYPL one of the five greatest research institutions in the world.

Astor Hall – In the white-marble foyer, just inside the Fifth Avenue entrance, you'll find information booths staffed by friendly volunteers.

South Court – A six-story glass structure with cantilevered floors holds the **visitor center**, where you can see a 12-minute film on the history of the library.

DeWitt Wallace Periodical Room – Rich wood paneling and 13 murals by 20C artist Richard Haas decorate this space.

Salomon Room★ *(3rd floor)* – This 19C picture gallery with rotating selections from the library's special collections includes a draft of the Declaration of Independence in Thomas Jefferson's own hand and an edition of Galileo's works that can only be read under a magnifying glass.

Main Reading Room★ *(3rd floor)* – The glorious space (half an acre), with its 51ft-high painted ceilings and rows of long oak tables dotted with green reading lamps, was meticulously preserved and updated in a $15 million renovation, completed in 1998.

Culture vultures, welcome to New York City, the cultural capital of the US! The number, quality and variety of museums in New York will truly boggle your mind. From medieval cloisters to modern tenements, New York has a museum to display it. As for art, let's talk world-class: the Met, MoMA, the Guggenheim . . . the list goes on and on.

American Museum of Natural History★★★

Central Park West between 77nd & 81st Sts. 212-769-5100. www.amnh.org. Open year-round daily 10am–5:45pm (Rose Center open until 8:45pm). $12 (includes admission to Rose Center exhibits). Closed Thanksgiving Day & Dec 25. B, C train to 81st St.; 1 or 9 train to 79th St.

If you think of natural history museums as places with case after glass case of beetles pinned onto cork board, this place will make you think again. A famed research facility, the institution works hard to bring up-to-date scientific techniques to its mammoth collection. The museum was founded in 1869, and the seed of the present facility (actually 23 connecting structures) was sown in 1874, when President Ulysses S. Grant laid the cornerstone of a hall designed by Calvert Vaux. Theodore Roosevelt, an ardent naturalist, gave the museum a bat, a turtle, four bird eggs, twelve mice and the skull of a red squirrel. The building underwent a renaissance in the 1990s with the renovation of its fourth-floor galleries and the construction of the Rose Center for Earth and Space *(see sidebar)*, opened in 2000. Still, only a small portion of the museum's 30 million artifacts and specimens, gathered from more than 1,000 globe-trotting expeditions, are on view at any given time.

Fossil Halls★★ – *Fourth floor.* This stunning new presentation includes 100 specimens laid out along the branches of the cladogram, or evolutionary tree, of life on Earth. The six halls here are dense with information, so it's best to begin your visit at the exhibit's orientation center.

• **Hall of Vertebrate Origins** – Follow the development of vertebrates from the earliest jawless fish to dinosaurs and mammals starting with this gallery.

Hall of Minerals and Gems★★ – *First floor*. Eye-popping galleries contain 6,000 specimens of rocks, minerals, meteorites and gems.

• The famed Star of India, the world's largest star sapphire, weighs 563 carats.

• The stunning Patricia Emerald tops out at a whopping 632 carats.

Hall of Asian Peoples★ – *Second floor*. Displays document life in Asia from prehistoric times to the late 19C. With more than 60,000 artifacts, the Asian collection is one of the largest of its kind in the Western Hemisphere.

> **Rose Center for Earth and Space**★★
>
> Gone is the old cement dome of the Hayden Planetarium. Now the Hayden Sphere sits like a luminous pearl in this 12-story glass jewel box on 81st Street. The **Hall of the Universe**★ is particularly dazzling, with a video feed from the Hubble Space Telescope and towering models of cosmic phenomena. One of Hollywood's biggest stars is in the virtual cockpit *(advance tickets: 212-769-5200)*.

Hall of Biodiversity★ – *First floor*. Here you'll be wowed by the variety and interactivity of life on earth.

• Walk through a **diorama** of an African rain forest.

Hall of Ocean Life – *First floor*. Reopened in summer 2003 after a $25 million renovation, the Hall of Ocean Life showcases dioramas of ocean environments and denizens ranging from a two-story coral reef to tiger sharks and a giant squid. The centerpiece of this hall is a 94ft model of a **blue whale** suspended in a dive position in an "ocean" created with lights, sound and video. The largest animal that ever lived, the blue whale *(Balaenoptera musculus)* can grow to a weight of 400,000 pounds. It feeds at ocean depths of 165–1,000ft, swallowing up to 17,000 gallons of water filled with shrimp-like krill at a time.

Hall of the Pacific Peoples★ – *Third floor*. Six cultural areas of the Pacific are represented here: Australia, Indonesia, the Philippines, Melanesia, Micronesia and Polynesia.

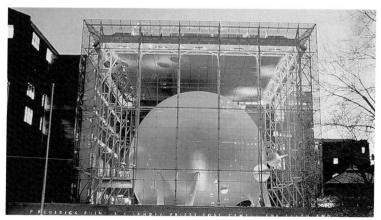

The Cloisters ★★★

Fort Tryon Park, between 190th & 200th Sts. from Broadway to the Hudson River. 212-923-3700. www.metmuseum.org. Open Mar–Oct Tue–Sun 9:30am–5:15pm, rest of the year Tue–Sun 9:30am–4:45pm. Closed Mon & major holidays. $12. A train to 190th St.-Overlook Terrace.

> **Unicorns!**
>
> The Cloisters' world-famous **unicorn tapestries**★ date from the late 15C and early 16C, the golden age of tapestry-making. The set of seven originally hung in a chateau belonging to the La Rochefoucauld family in southern France. The story the tapestries tell, of the unicorn being hunted and born again, may be a parable for the crucifixion of Christ.

The Cloisters offers one of New York's most serene museum experiences. Built on a hilltop in a park overlooking the Hudson, the compound incorporates architectural treasures from Europe, including four cloisters (quadrangles surrounded by covered walkways, or arcades), to create what looks like a fortified monastery. Within are 5,000 pieces from the Metropolitan Museum's stellar collection of medieval art, very much in their element. The core of the collection was put together by the American sculptor George Grey Barnard (1863–1938) and was first presented to the public in 1914. In 1925 oil scion John D. Rockefeller donated 40 medieval

sculptures to the Met, along with the money to buy Barnard's collection. Five years later he presented the city of New York with an estate he owned in northern Manhattan (now Fort Tryon Park), provided that the north end of the property be reserved for the Cloisters. The site is lovely to visit on a nice day, when you can watch sunlight filter in through the many treasured stained-glass windows.

Main Floor

- **Cuxa Cloister**, from a 12C monastery in the French Pyrenees, is the largest in the complex, but is only half the size of the original.

- **Fuentidueña Chapel**, devoted to Spanish Romanesque art, flanks the Cuxa Cloister.

- The walkway of the **Saint-Guilhem Cloister,** from Montpellier, France, contains a magnificent series of 12C–13C columns and capitals.

- **Campin Room** contains the famous **Annunciation Triptych** by the 15C Flemish artist Robert Campin.

Ground Floor

- Petite **Trie Cloister**, with its 15C capitals and fountain, is particularly meditative.

- The 13C–14C **Bonnefort Cloister** contains a garden of medieval herbs and flowers.

- The **Gothic Chapel** makes a superb setting for a collection of tomb effigies and slabs.

- The **treasury** displays the Cloisters' collection of smaller objects, including an outstanding walrus-ivory cross from the 12C, and the magnificent *Book of Hours* manuscript.

Frick Collection★★★

Fifth Ave. at 70th St. 212-288-0700. www.frick.org. Open year-round Tue–Sat 10am–6pm (Fri until 9pm), Sun 1pm–6pm. Closed Mon & major holidays. $12. 6 train to 68th St.

For a mellow glimpse at the spoils of the Gilded Age, look no farther than the Frick. Like many of his fellow robber barons, Pittsburgh steel and railroad tycoon Henry Clay Frick developed a taste for art, and he bought this collection of paintings, furnishings, sculpture and china (which spans the 14C–19C), including some exceptional Dutch masters, over the course of four decades. In 1913, at the age of 64, Frick commissioned Carrère and Hastings to build a 40-room manse for his holdings (and himself); he took up residence here in 1914 and died five years later. Since the museum's opening in 1919, the building has been expanded twice and the collection has grown by a third. Today 16 galleries are on view.

Fragonard Room – Eleven decorative paintings by the 18C artist Jean-Honoré Fragonard, including four depicting the "progress of love," are complemented by exquisite 18C French furniture and Sèvres porcelain.

Living Hall – Masterpieces by Holbein, Titian, El Greco and Bellini share space with furnishings by the famous 17C French cabinetmaker André-Charles Boulle.

West Gallery – Landscapes by Constable, Ruisdael and Corot, among others, hang alongside portraits by Rembrandt *(Self-Portrait)* and Velázquez *(Philip IV of Spain)* in the house's largest gallery.

Enamel Room – Piero della Francesca's image of St. John the Evangelist is the only large painting by Piero in the US. Note also the splendid collection of Limoges painted enamels dating from the 16C–17C.

East Gallery – The room includes four portraits by Whistler, two by Goya, and two by Van Dyck, as well as the collection's only still life, Chardin's *Still Life with Plums*.

Frick Facts

Because its works aren't trapped behind glass or cordoned off by velvet ropes, the Frick doesn't allow any children under 10 inside. Audio tours are free with admission, as is a good orientation film, shown in the Music Room on the half-hour. Like many other New York museums, the Frick has recently expanded its hours. Consider visiting on a Friday night between 6:30pm and 9pm, when the lovely skylit Garden Court hosts a cash bar.

Museums

The Metropolitan Museum of Art★★★

Fifth Ave. at 82nd St. 212-879-5500. www.metmuseum.org. Open year-round Tue–Sun 9:30am–5:30pm (Fri & Sat until 9pm). Closed Mon & major holidays. $10 (includes same-day admission to The Cloisters). 4, 5 or 6 train to 86th St.

Art lovers from around the world flock to the Met, the biggest museum in the Western Hemisphere. The collection embraces three million objects tracing 5,000 years of human history, so you can spend a day studying one period or get a primer on all of art history. The museum has humble origins: Founded in 1870, it opened in a dancing academy in 1872. In 1880 it moved to its present location, but its signature Beaux-Arts facade, designed by Richard Morris Hunt, wasn't completed until 1902. Actually, it was never finished. Look atop the twinned columns—those chunky blocks were supposed to be carved. Alas. A master plan drawn up for the museum's centennial celebration in 1970 called for an ambitious expansion. Wings and courtyards built through the 1990s complemented the Met's traditional exhibition halls with space for, among other things, a massive Egyptian temple (Temple of Dendur) and the personal collection of a Wall Street mogul (Lehman Pavilion).

Meet The Met

The Met has been called an encyclopedia of the arts, so don't go in expecting to read it cover to cover. The "Director's Selections" audio tour *(rent equipment in the Great Hall)*, which traces the history of art through 58 masterworks, is one way to approach the collection. Another is by taking a free guided tour *(offered daily; call or check Web site for schedule)*. The Met is usually hosting at least one blockbuster traveling show as well, focusing on a particular school or artist. Or you can just explore your favorite areas: a single wing can take a whole day to appreciate.

Best of The Met

American Wing★★★ – Twenty-five period rooms show off decorative arts from the Jacobean style through the work of Chippendale, Duncan Phyfe and Frank Lloyd Wright. Painting highlights include masterworks of the Hudson River School and high-society portraits by John Singer Sargent. The sunlit Charles Engelhard Court displays Tiffany art-glass lamps and silverware.

Ancient Art★★★ – The Egyptian wing is a perennial favorite, its 69,000sq ft of exhibition space (jewels, funerary art) ending in the glass-enclosed Temple of Dendur. On the other side of the Met, eight newly renovated galleries for Greek and Roman art display architectural fragments, statues, vases, bronzework and sarcophagi. The final phase of renovation work is under way.

European Sculpture and Decorative Arts★★★ – This is one of the museum's largest departments, with more than 60,000 works from the Renaissance to the early 20C. Pieces are displayed in exquisitely re-created period rooms.

13C–18C European Paintings★★★ Paintings on the 2nd floor include works by Titian, Raphael, Tiepolo, El Greco, Velázquez, Thomas Gainsborough and others. The museum owns 20 paintings by Rembrandt.

Drinking It All In

With 2 million square feet of exhibition space, the Met can be hard on the old gams. So take a load off at one of its scattered cafes. The biggest, a subterranean cafeteria under the ancient art galleries, opened in June 2003 and offers a pasta bar, wraps, salads and the like. The Petrie European Sculpture Court hosts a coffee and wine bar with a view of Central Park. During the warm months, the Roof Garden Cafe serves up light snacks, contemporary sculpture and dazzling scenery. The Great Hall Balcony Bar has live music every day from 5pm to 8pm.

19C European Paintings and Sculpture★★★ – Designed in the Beaux-Arts style, these 21 galleries provide a luscious backdrop for works spanning the 19C. It was a fertile century, and the Met traces its evolution from the Neoclassicism of J.A.D. Ingres to the tempestuous work of Vincent Van Gogh.

Arts of Africa, Oceania and the Americas★★ – These spacious galleries full of stunning totem poles, masks, shields and sculpture are dedicated to Michael Rockefeller, the oil scion who died on an anthropological visit to New Guinea in 1961.

Lehman Pavilion★★ – Shown in rotating exhibits, the 3,000-work collection is most famous for its 14C and 15C Italian paintings.

Medieval Art★★ – Complementing the collection at the Cloisters, 6,000 works of Byzantine silver, Romanesque and Gothic metalwork, stained glass and tapestries can be found in moody galleries, including a cryptlike space under the stairs of the Great Hall.

Costume Institute★ – With recent homages to Jackie Kennedy and rock-and-roll style, the Costume Institute is a magnet for fashion victims.

Museum of Modern Art (MoMA) ★★★

45-20 33rd St. at Queens Blvd. 212-708-9400. www.moma.org. Open year-round Thu–Mon 10am–5pm (Fri until 7:45pm). Closed Tue, Wed & major holidays. $12. 7 train to 33rd St.

Yes, it takes a bit more effort to get to MoMA these days—it has been moved out to Queens while its Midtown digs undergo a major expansion and renovation—but the trip is worth it. As you arrive by the elevated 7 train you're treated to a trompe-l'oeil: a set of painted equipment boxes on the roof of the old Swingline Stapler Factory, the museum's temporary home, appear in abstract formation, briefly co-alesce to spell "MoMA," then disappear again into abstraction.

The museum was founded in 1929 by three rich, forward-thinking women—Abby Aldrich Rockefeller (whose husband, John D. Jr., hated modern art), Lillie P. Bliss, and Mary Quinn Sullivan. Their first show, featuring the little-known post-Impressionists, opened in temporary quarters that fall. Over the next decade, founding director Alfred H. Barr Jr. shaped MoMA's philosophy. Not only did he mount shows of contemporary paintings that didn't yet have the art establishment's seal of approval; he also exhibited photography, architecture and design, none of which were considered legitimate art forms at the time. The design of the museum's headquarters, opened in 1939, could have come right out of Barr's groundbreaking 1932 show "Modern Architecture: International Exhibition," in which he coined the term "International style." Since then MoMA's holdings have grown to encompass more than 100,000 pieces and 19,000 films.

Alfred Barr pioneered the concept of a multidepartmental museum of art. Today MoMA's great works are divided into six main categories. Though only a small fraction of them will be on display in Queens, this overview will give you

---

A New Home

As MoMA's collection grew, its 1939 home underwent two expansions, one by Philip Johnson in 1964 and another by Cesar Pelli in 1979. But the latest, by Yoshio Taniguchi, is the largest and most ambitious. Scheduled to reopen in 2005, the new MoMA will feature 630,000sq ft of space. Two structures will frame an enlarged Abby Aldrich Rockefeller Sculpture Garden: a new gallery building and a stand-alone Education and Research Center. They will be joined by a grand pedestrian thoroughfare. Other highlights include larger, more flexible spaces for contemporary art, and architecturally distinctive galleries for the museum's masterpieces.

a sense of the museum's holdings—and why MoMA needs to expand to properly display them.

Architecture and Design – MoMA established the world's first curatorial department devoted to architecture and design in 1932. Today the design collection comprises more than 3,000 objects, ranging from a Bic pen to a Bell helicopter, as well as 4,000 examples of typography. The architecture collection documents buildings through models, drawings and photographs.

Drawings – More than 6,000 works on paper include studies and completed drawings by Degas, Cézanne, Picasso, Matisse, Klee, Schwitters, Kandinsky, Jean Arp, Georgia O'Keeffe and Ellsworth Kelly.

Film and Media – The museum's film library was founded in 1935 and now incorporates all periods and genres. Among the holdings are original negatives of the Biograph and Edison companies, and the world's largest collection of D.W. Griffith films. During the renovation, films can be seen at the Gramercy Theatre *(127 E. 23rd St. in Manhattan; 212-777-4900)*.

Painting and Sculpture – MoMA's bread and butter, this is the world's largest and most inclusive collection of modern painting and sculpture; it numbers 3,200 works from the late 19C to the present. Masterpieces include Van Gogh's *Starry Night*, Cézanne's *Bather,* Picasso's *Desmoiselles d'Avignon,* Henri Rousseau's *Dream,* Frida Kahlo's *Self-Portrait with Cropped Hair,* Salvador Dali's *Persistence of Memory,* and installations by Louise Bourgeois and Rachel Whiteread. Rotating "greatest hits" selections are always on view at MoMA Queens.

Photography – The museum owns 25,000 works by the likes of shutterbugs Man Ray, Paul Strand, Edward Weston, Dorothea Lange, Weegee, Ansel Adams, Robert Frank and Cindy Sherman.

Prints and Illustrated Books – Some 50,000 works range from prints by Toulouse-Lautrec and Edvard Munch to Jenny Holzer's photostat *Truisms.*

Queens Artlink

On weekends a free shuttle bus runs between the MoMA construction site at West 53rd Street and MoMA QNS. Another bus connects MoMA QNS to other Queens cultural destinations, including MoMA partner P.S. 1 *(see Boroughs/Queens). For schedule, call 212-708-9750 or visit www.queensartlink.org.*

Ellis Island Immigration Museum ★★

On Ellis Island in New York Harbor. 212-363-3200. www.ellisisland.com. Open year-round daily 9:30am–5pm. Closed Dec 25.

Hate waiting in lines? Imagine being among the 5,000 newly arrived immigrants who were processed here daily between 1900 and 1924. Lying halfway between Manhattan and Liberty Island, Ellis Island is the 27.5-acre parcel that served as a gateway for 12 million immigrants seeking a new life in the US. Today the powerful site, a natural companion to the Statue of Liberty, describes the grueling inspection process and commemorates immigrants' courage. In 1892 the first Ellis Island immigration facility opened, but the main reception hall burned down in 1897. It was replaced in 1900 by the present building, a stunning French Renaissance concoction of limestone and brick by architects William Boring and Edward Tilton.

The number of immigrants who were processed here hit a peak of 11,747 during one day in 1907. Indeed, 100 million Americans can trace their lineage through Ellis Island. Restrictive laws and quotas passed in the wake of World War I cut immigration to a trickle, and in 1954 the facility was officially closed. The island was declared part of the Statue of Liberty National Monument in 1965, but it was not until 1984 that a six-year, $162 million restoration program began. Reopened in 1990, the 200,000sq ft Ellis Island Immigration Museum is the only one of the island's 33 structures accessible to the public.

First floor – Visitors coming off the ferry enter the baggage room, where immigrants were separated, sometimes forever, from their belongings.

Second floor – The sweeping Registry Room/Great Hall, capped with a vaulted ceiling of 28,000 interlocking tiles, was the site of initial inspections. It now stands empty.

Third floor – Exhibits include keepsakes from immigrants and their families, and a dorm room re-creating the cramped conditions of life on the island.

Visiting Ellis Island

See Statue of Liberty entry in Must-See Landmarks for ferry information. Free tickets to the 30-minute documentary *Island of Hope/Island of Fears* are distributed on a first-come, first-served basis; shows fill up quickly, so pick yours up as soon as you arrive. The museum's newest service is an online database containing the passenger records of all the ships that landed at Ellis Island: terminals are available at the museum, or online at www.ellisisland.org.

Forbes Galleries★★

62 Fifth Ave. 212-206-5548. Open year-round Tue–Sat 10am–4pm. Closed Sun, Mon, Thu & major holidays. Any train to 14th St./Union Square.

If you're south of 14th Street and have a craving for Fabergé eggs, make sure to stop in at the Forbes Galleries. This eclectic little museum—there are only seven rooms—is housed in the ground floor of the Forbes Building; upper floors contain the offices of the business magazine of the same name. The structure itself, completed in 1925, has a notable pedigree: It was designed by Carrère and Hastings, architects of the New York Public Library and the Frick mansion, in association with Shreve and Lamb, who later designed the Empire State Building. The galleries were opened in 1985 and reflect the wide-ranging interests of publisher **Malcolm Forbes** (1919–1990) and his sons.

Fabergé Room – Treasures in this room (actually a high-security vault) include not only the famous eggs, but 300 other jeweled works, from gold knitting needles embedded with rubies to a luxurious crown sparkling with diamonds.

Toy and Trophy Room – Here you'll find 500 toy boats, the largest flotilla of its kind in the country, along with 12,000 **miniature soldiers**, some of the oldest Monopoly sets in the world, and a wide assortment of antique trophies.

Picture and Autograph Galleries – Rare manuscripts, including Abraham Lincoln's Emancipation Proclamation, are on view, along with a selection of other presidential memorabilia, including the opera glasses Lincoln was holding when he was assassinated.

What's In An Egg?

Forbes encountered the work of Russian jeweler **Peter Carl Fabergé** when he purchased a gold cigarette case for his wife. Soon he became one of the world's preeminent collectors of Fabergé's luxurious whimsies, purchasing, among other things, 12 of the 45 Imperial Easter Eggs Fabergé's workshop made for the last two Russian czars. Gold, silver, precious stones and enameling decorate these exquisite bonbons, several of which conceal hidden surprises: A mechanical bird emerges and sings when a certain orange is rotated on the Orange Tree Egg, and a rooster appears every hour on the hour, crowing and flapping its wings, on the Chanticleer Egg.

Guggenheim Museum★★

1071 Fifth Ave. between 88th & 9th Sts. 212-423-3500. www.guggenheim.org. Open Fri–Wed 10am–5:45pm (Fri until 8pm). Closed Thu & major holidays. $15. 4, 5 or 6 train to 86th St.

Frank Lloyd Wright's spiraling Modernist statement—one of the most original buildings in the US—is reason enough to check out the Guggenheim, also home to some fine modern and contemporary art. **Solomon R. Guggenheim** (1861–1949), heir to a vast mining fortune, started his collection with Old Masters, but in the early 20C shifted his focus to nonrepresentational art. In 1943 Frank Lloyd Wright was commissioned to design a permanent home for Guggenheim's collection. Wright was an outspoken critic of New York architecture, and the city returned the favor by blasting his design. The 1959 structure, an idiosyncratic design based on a complex trigonometric spiral, clashed with the sedate brownstones of the Upper East Side and was a nightmare to construct. Worse, its interior ramp and sloping walls made presenting and viewing art difficult, if not impossible. Wright considered it his crowning achievement. In 1992 a 10-story limestone annex was built behind the structure, with ramps leading from Wright's nautilus into its more hospitable gallery spaces.

Collection – The Guggenheim Foundation owns about 6,000 paintings, sculptures and works on paper. Core holdings comprise 195 works by Wassily Kandinsky—the largest group of his work in the US—and more than 75 pieces by Klee, Chagall, Delaunay, Dubuffet and Mondrian. However, the only works permanently on display are selections from the **Thannhauser Collection**★ of late-19C and early-20C art, including paintings by Picasso, Cézanne, Degas, Manet, Pissarro and van Gogh. The rest of the museum is devoted to temporary shows.

Guggenheim Goes Global

The Guggenheim has seen the value in expanding. It has also learned the risks. After the museum opened its hugely successful Bilbao outpost, designed by Frank Gehry, in 1997, hundreds of cities clamored for a Guggenheim of their own. Berlin, Venice and Las Vegas each got one; then the money dried up. In 2002 Guggenheim SoHo closed, and plans for a Gehry-designed pile on the southern tip of Manhattan were scrapped. Staff was cut in half, and talks of Edinburgh, Tokyo and Salzburg spaces ended. The rough patch might be over, though: in May 2003 the mayor of Rio de Janeiro signed on for a waterfront Guggenheim. It will open in 2007.

Museum of the City of New York★★

Fifth Ave. at 103rd St. 212-534-1672. www.mcny.org. Open year-round Wed–Sat 10am–5pm, Sun noon–5pm. Closed Mon, Tue & major holidays. $7. 6 train to 103rd St.

The Museum of the City of New York chronicles the Big Apple's growth from Dutch trading post to thriving metropolis with period rooms, galleries, and historical exhibits. Founded in 1923, the museum first resided at Gracie Mansion. It moved to the current location, a Georgian Revival building fronting Central Park, in 1929. Since then the collection has grown to encompass more than 1.5 million paintings, prints, photographs, costumes, toys, rare books, manuscripts, sculptures, decorative art objects and other artifacts. For years the museum has been hankering to move downtown, but plans to occupy the refurbished Tweed Courthouse fell through in 2002 when Mayor Michael Bloomberg turned the building over to the Department of Education instead. So the search continues.

Period Alcoves – On the second floor, six period alcoves chart the history of New York interiors, from a 17C Dutch living room to a late-19C drawing room.

Silver – The most complete collection of New York silver, including tea services and mongrammed tankards, spans three centuries.

Marine Collection – The history of maritime New York is told through 100 scale-model ships, more than 100 paintings, figureheads and nautical instruments.

Toys – The assemblage of more than 10,000 toys used by New Yorkers from the Colonial period to the present, includes a series of exquisite **dollhouses**★.

Rockefeller Interiors – Two ornate rooms from John D. Rockefeller's 1860s residence reflect the opulent tastes of the late Victorian era.

"Engravings for the People"

Very few New Yorkers in the 19C had the time or the money to sit for portraits, but many wanted tasteful decorations for their homes. Currier and Ives to the rescue! Founded in 1835 by 21-year-old Nathaniel Currier of Massachusetts, the company churned out three or four original designs each week for 50 years. The factory on Spruce Street bustled with artists, lithographers, letterers and colorists; the Nassau Street shop was a meeting place for newspapermen, who placed Currier and Ives political cartoons and illustrations in their papers. By the time the firm closed in 1907 it had produced 7,000 images that had been reproduced by the million. The museum's collection of 2,800 original hand-painted lithographs is the finest and most complete such archive in existence.

National Museum of the American Indian★★

[M1] *refers to map on inside front cover. 1 Bowling Green. 212-514-3700. www.american indian.si.edu. Open year-round daily 10am–5pm (Thu until 8pm). Closed Dec 25. 4 or 5 train to Bowling Green.*

This Smithsonian Institution treasure trove of Native American art and artifacts was established by an act of Congress in 1994 to protect and foster the heritage and cultures of the Native people of the Americas. (A companion museum is scheduled to open in 2004 on the National Mall in Washington, DC.) Its home is the second floor of the Alexander Hamilton US Custom House, a Beaux-Arts gem by Minnesota architect Cass Gilbert. Rising seven stories, the structure is ringed with 44 columns, each decorated with a head of Mercury, the god of commerce. On the building's huge entrance pedestals are four large sculptures—seated female figures representing America, Asia, Europe and Africa—by Daniel Chester French. Inside, shells, nautical figures and sea creatures form part of the decoration, recalling New York's history as an important port. The murals on the magnificent rotunda dome—one series depicts American settlers, the other a ship coming into New York Harbor—were painted by celebrated New York artist Reginald Marsh in 1937.

The Galleries – Currently on display, an ongoing exhibition of work by contemporary Native American artists runs through November 2004.

George Gustav Heye

A native New Yorker, Heye (1874–1957) studied engineering at Columbia and had a short career as an investment banker, but his real passion was collecting. Over the course of 45 years, he gathered almost a million objects from indigenous peoples throughout the Western Hemisphere. Unlike most collectors, who try to single out only significant objects for purchase, on his trips to American Indian communities Heye would simply buy everything in sight. His first acquisition was an Apache deerskin shirt, which he acquired in 1897 while on a railroad construction job in Arizona. In 1916 he founded the Museum of the American Indian, which operated from 1922 to 1994 at 155th Street and Broadway.

New-York Historical Society★★

2 W. 77th St. at Central Park West. 212-873-3400. www.nyhistory.org. Open year-round Tue–Sun 10am–6pm. Closed Mon. $6. B or C train to 81st St.; 1 or 9 train to 79th St.

It may be New York's oldest museum, but curators at the historical society approach its rich trove of material with a keenly modern eye. The acclaimed **Henry Luce Center for the Study of American Culture**★, which opened in November 2000, is especially fun to explore. Presented in what's called "working storage" format, nearly 40,000 objects are on view, and you need only press a button to get an entertaining rundown (sometimes from a celebrity) on each piece's place in history. The society was founded in 1804 with a mission to preserve the history of the US, and since then it has amassed a collection that embraces three centuries of Americana, with a special focus on New York material from the late 1700s to the early 1900s. The present Neoclassical building was opened in 1908 after the society outgrew its first home in the East Village; it was renovated in the late 1990s and again in 2003.

First Floor – Four large galleries are devoted to temporary exhibits, many of which are culled from the society's extensive collections.

Second Floor – Thomas Cole's five-painting series *The Course of Empire* and other works by Hudson River school artists are displayed salon-style along with smaller landscapes and portraiture by Rembrandt Peale and others.

Fourth Floor – The Luce Center's holdings range from George Washington's camp bed at Valley Forge to the world's largest collection of Tiffany lamps, with thousands of odds and ends in between. A browser's delight.

History Responds

The society's latest role has been to serve as the primary repository of artifacts relating to the September 11, 2001 attack on the World Trade Center and to interpret the material in a series of programs called "History Responds." A portion of a fire truck from Brooklyn's Rescue Two, a piece of a police car, gear worn in the rescue and clean-up effort, charred papers, shards of glass, a violently contorted Venetian blind (found in a tree), and even vials of dust and debris, gathered instinctively in the aftermath, have become part of this chilling new collection.

Pierpont Morgan Library★★

29 E. 36th St. at Madison Ave. 212-685-0610. morganlibrary.org. Closed until early 2006 (see sidebar). 4, 5 or 6 train to 33rd St.

To see Beethoven's Violin Sonata No. 10 in G Major as it emerged from the composer's pen is to glimpse a mind furiously, engagingly at work. The Morgan has thousands of such documents. The collection grew out of the personal holdings of **Pierpont Morgan** (1837–1913), a wealthy financier and patron of the arts. In 1902 he commissioned the noted firm McKim, Mead, and White to build a home for his growing "library." The Italian Renaissance main building, constructed of Tennessee marble blocks laid up without mortar, was completed in 1906 and opened to the public after Morgan's death in 1913. An annex was added in 1928. The third building on the site, the brownstone where Pierpont Morgan's son J.P. once lived, dates to 1852. In 2002 the $10 million Thaw Conservation Center opened on the fourth floor of the brownstone, offering state-of-the-art facilities to researchers and archivists.

Bigger and Better

In May 2003 the library closed to the general public in order to carry out an ambitious expansion and renovation. Pritzker-winning architect Renzo Piano's master plan, unanimously approved by the New York City Landmarks Preservation Commission, involves the construction of three glass-and-steel pavilions between the three existing structures. The project not only better unifies the complex, it expands gallery space by a third. The work should take two and a half years.

Collection Highlights

- More than 15,000 prints and drawings, including works by Blake, Degas, Dürer, Pollock, Pontormo, Rubens and Watteau
- The country's largest and finest collection of Rembrandt etchings
- Ten centuries of Western illumination are represented by nearly 1,300 manuscripts as well as papyri
- Three Gutenberg Bibles
- Manuscripts of Charles Dickens' *Christmas Carol* and Henry David Thoreau's journals
- Original handwritten works by Bach, Brahms, Schubert and Stravinsky
- Letters from Mozart, Jane Austen, Charlotte Brontë, Albert Einstein, Abraham Lincoln, John Steinbeck and Voltaire

Whitney Museum of American Art★★

945 Madison Ave. at 74th St. 212-570-3676 or 800-944-8639. www.whitney.org. Open year-round Tue–Sun 11am–6pm (Fri until 9pm). Closed Mon & major holidays. $12. 6 train to 77th St.

A diehard champion of emerging artists, the Whitney also has one of the world's best collections of 20C American art. The museum grew out of the personal art collection of sculptor and art collector **Gertrude Vanderbilt Whitney** (1875–1942), the rebellious daughter of railroad titan Cornelius Vanderbilt. After starting the Whitney Art Club in her Greenwich Village studio, she began to acquire works by living American artists, including painters Edward Hopper, Willem de Kooning, Ellsworth Kelly and Robert Motherwell, as well as sculptors Alexander Calder, Louise Nevelson and Isamu Noguchi. Her holdings outgrew two homes, moving to this, its third, in 1966.

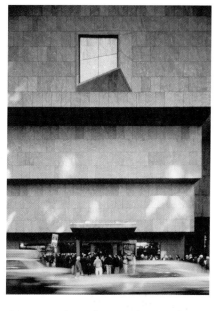

The stark granite structure by Marcel Breuer and Hamilton Smith is cantilevered over a sunken sculpture garden.

Permanent Collection – Now comprising 10,000 works, the Whitney's holdings are displayed in rotating exhibits on the second and fifth floors. Count on finding masterworks from the first half of the 20C (Marsden Hartley, Georgia O'Keeffe) along with postwar and contemporary artists (Jackson Pollock, Kiki Smith, Andy Warhol).

Temporary Exhibits – The museum's frequently changing exhibits explore daring, innovative and often controversial topics. In recent years film, video, installation art and mixed media have become popular forms.

Loving To Hate It

Every two years the Whitney Museum presents a selection of what it believes is the most noteworthy American art. Every two years critics sharpen their tongues and say it's the worst show yet. The inaugural biennial of 1932 bespoke "the deplorable state of American art," according to the *New York Herald Tribune*. "Pretentious mediocrity, vulgarity, and insignificance," sniffed *The Nation* in 1946. "A kind of instant junkyard of the future" was the *Times'* take on the 1969 show, and in 1993 the *New York Observer* predicted there was "no cure in sight." Debra Singer, the co-curator of the 2004 show, says the negative reviews have an upside. They are so predictable that she feels "no pressure at all" to please anyone.

Cooper-Hewitt National Design Museum★

2 E. 91st St. at Fifth Ave. 212-849-8400. www.ndm.si.edu. Open year-round Tue–Fri 10am–5pm (Tue until 9pm), Sat 10am–6pm, Sun noon–5pm. Closed Mon & major holidays. $8. 4, 5 or 6 train to 86th or 96th Sts.

Magazine covers, measuring cups, homeless shelters, automobiles, typefaces, condominiums and chromosome models were just a few of the objects turned inside-out at the Cooper-Hewitt's National Design Triennial of 2003. By celebrating contemporary and historic design in this and other shows, the museum proves how everyday things can be reimagined and enhanced. The Cooper-Hewitt was founded in 1897 by New York socialites Sarah, Eleanor, and Amy Hewitt—granddaughters of industrialist Peter Cooper—as part of the Cooper Union for the Advancement of Science; since 1967 the museum has been affiliated with the Smithsonian Institution. Changing exhibits fill the vast galleries of Andrew Carnegie's 1898 château-style manse, whose grounds include a delightful garden.

Permanent Collection – The trove of more than 250,000 objects is one of the largest repositories of design in the world. It has 10,000 different wallpaper samples and a sketch by Michelangelo, as well as drawings by Frank Lloyd Wright and fabrics dating back to 200 BC. You have to make an appointment to see such works, but you don't need any special credentials to do so.

International Center of Photography★

[M2] *refers to map on inside front cover. 1133 Avenue of the Americas (Sixth Ave.) at 43nd St. 212-857-0000. www.icp.org. Open year-round Tue–Fri 10am–5pm (Fri until 8pm), weekends 10am–6pm. Closed Mon & major holidays. $9. Any train to 42nd St.*

"Concerned photography" forms the heart of the collection here, though there is little that is sentimental about this place. The ICP, as it is known, was founded in 1974 by Cornell Capa, whose brother Robert took dramatic photos of the fighting during the Spanish Civil War and World War II. Since then the museum's holdings have grown to encompass 60,000 prints, with a special strength on documentary and reportage of that type. Yet there is plenty of room for beauty, scandal and whimsy as well. The ICP's vaults also include work by the fashion photographer David Seidner, whose portraits beautifully mimic the composition of the Old Masters, and Henri Cartier-Bresson, who took most of his pictures with a tiny Leica. Recent shows (all the displays are temporary) have featured photographic portraits by author Lewis Carroll; contemporary images of Cuba; and historical pictures of Harlem and Chicago.

Weegee's World

The tabloid photographer Weegee used his flashbulb to expose New York City's dark side—if his subjects weren't drunk, they were usually dead. How did he get the shot? By installing a police radio in his car— that way he could be the first to arrive at crime scenes, recording all the grisly details for the morning papers. His scandal-sheet images from the 1930s and 1940s are now legendary. The ICP owns 13,000 of Weegee's prints, tear-sheets, negatives and manuscripts—the biggest archive of his work in the world.

Lower East Side Tenement Museum★

90 and 97 Orchard St. 212-431-0233. www.tenement.org. Visitor center open daily 11am–5pm, tenement building open Tue–Fri 1pm–4pm, weekends 11am–4:30pm; Confino Family Apt open weekends only noon–3pm. Ticket prices vary according to tour, age, and time of week. F train to Delancey St.

Even by New York standards, the apartments at 97 Orchard Street are small. Yet throughout the late 19C and early 20C, these tiny dwellings hosted wave after wave of immigrant families. Those immigrants' experiences—working a lot, sleeping a little, getting to know their neighbors all too well—are the very essence of New York City, so this museum decided to memorialize them. If these walls could talk, the founders seemed to ask of this 1860s tenement, what would they say? The answer comes through in three apartments that have been restored and furnished to reflect the lives and tastes of former occupants: the German-born Gumpertzes (1878), the Rogarshevsky family of Lithuania (1921), and the Baldizzis of Sicily (1935). Keepsakes, photographs and newspaper clippings flesh out their stories. The fact that these residents represent only a handful of the 7,000 people who coursed through 97 Orchard between 1865 and 1935 merely makes you more curious about the others.

Tips For Visiting

Docent-led tours of the tenement (the only way to see it) leave daily every half-hour from 90 Orchard Street, the museum's visitor center. You can purchase same-day tickets there, but tours often sell out. To buy tickets in advance, call 800-965-4827 or log on to the museum's Web site, which also has a complete tour schedule. If you're traveling with kids, consider taking the smaller, "living history" tour of the Confino family apartment *(see Musts for Kids)*. New tours on the garment industry and living through the economic depressions of 1873 and 1929 are also worth exploring.

Museum of Arts & Design★

[M3] refers to map on inside front cover. 40 W. 53rd St. 212-956-3535. www.madmuseum.org. Open year-round daily 10am–6pm (Thu until 8pm). Closed major holidays. $8. E or V train to 5th Ave./53rd St.

Formerly the American Craft Museum, the institution changed its name in 2002 because it felt the word "craft" had lost its oomph. Well, the museum hasn't. Since the facility's inauguration in 1956, it has become a top venue for both traditional and contemporary design, reporting a 100 percent increase in visitors in the past five years. Here you'll find rotating selections from the permanent collection of 2,000 works, as well as traveling exhibits. Recent shows have included work by Czech glass artist Stanislav Libensky and his students; Native American ceramics, glass, textiles, jewelry, metalwork, sculpture and mixed media; and quilts from six continents. The museum is currently housed in a mottled-pink office tower—the gallery within is a soaring atrium with a Guggenheim-esque spiral staircase—but it will move to Two Columbus Circle in 2006.

A New Home

Some people think that Two Columbus Circle looks like a parking garage. Others have compared its Venetian arcade to a line of lollipops. Made of marble with an almost windowless facade (despite its potentially great view of Central Park, right across the street), the building is certainly distinctive. The structure was designed by Edward Durrell Stone in 1964 for the Huntington Hartford Gallery of Contemporary Art. It passed through several hands, most recently the city's, before being abandoned in 1998. The museum snatched it up in mid-2002 for an undisclosed amount. Brad Cloepfil of Allied Works Architecture has been hired to do the redesign.

Neue Galerie★

1048 Fifth Ave. at 86th St. 212-628-6200. www.neuegalerie.org. Open year-round Fri–Mon 11am–6pm (Fri until 9pm). Closed Tue–Thu & major holidays. $10. 4, 5 or 6 train to 86th St.

Cosmetics mogul Ronald Lauder established the Neue Galerie in 2001 to display his and his art-dealer friend Serge Sabarsky's collections of early-20C Austrian and German art. The museum's name derives from the Neue Galerie of Vienna, founded in 1923, which encouraged the work of Gustav Klimt, Egon Schiele and others of the Secessionist movement. The muse-um's home, a Louis XIII-style Beaux-Arts mansion built in 1914 by Carrère and Hastings, has known some illustrious owners—it was once the residence of Mrs. Cornelius Vanderbilt III. It retains much of the grandeur of its society days and, in its new function, fits right in with the other architectural grand dames of Fifth Avenue's Museum Mile. Two temporary exhibitions a year will comple-ment rotating selections from the first-rate permanent collection.

Austrian Art – Second-floor galleries are arranged around a central staircase and landing, providing a sumptuous backdrop to work by Klimt, Schiele, Oskar Kokoschka and others.

Cafe Sabarsky

Linzertorte, anyone? In the lobby of the museum, this charming cafe re-creates the Viennese coffeehouses that nurtured intellectual and artistic life at the turn of the 20C. It is decorated with period objects and features a wide selection of Austrian pastries.

German Art – Peruse paintings by Kandinsky, Klee, Emil Nolde, Otto Dix, George Grosz and decorative arts by Bauhaus heavyweights Mies van der Rohe and Marcel Breuer on the third floor.

Museums

The Rest of the Best: NYC Museums

Asia Society ★ – *725 Park Ave. between 70th & 71st Sts. 212-517-2742. www.asiasociety.org. Open year-round Tues–Sun 11am–6pm (Fri until 9pm). Closed Mon & major holidays. $7. 6 train to 68th St.*
Founded in 1956 by John D. Rockefeller III to promote appreciation of Asian cultures, the museum houses more than 300 works, including bronzes, paintings, ceramics and sculpture from 2000 BC to the 1800s.

Audubon Terrace ★ – *Broadway between 155th & 156th St. Open year-round Tue–Sat 10am–4:30pm, Sun 1pm–4pm. Closed Mon & major holidays. 1 train to 157th St. or B train to 155th St.*
Naturalist John Audubon once had a country house and farm called Minniesland here. Today some of the city's lesser-known museums and cultural institutions, including the **American Academy of Arts and Letters** *(212-368-5900; open during exhibitions Mar & mid-May–mid-June Thu–Sun 1pm–4pm)* call this Beaux-Arts complex home.

• **Hispanic Society of America** ★★ – *212-926-2234. www.hispanicsociety.org. Same hours as Audubon Terrace.* The society boasts an impressive cache of Old Masters, including works by Goya, El Greco, Morales and Velásquez.

• **American Numismatic Society** ★ – *212-234-3130. www.amnumsoc.org. Same hours as Audubon Terrace.* The history of money is recounted through one of the world's foremost collection of coins.

Gracie Mansion ★ – *East End Ave. at 89th St. 212-570-4751. Visit by guided tour only, (reservations required) late Mar–mid-Nov, Wed 10am, 11am, 1pm, and 2 pm. $4. 4, 5 or 6 train to 86th St.*
Billionaire mayor Michael Bloomberg chose to remain in his East Side townhouse rather than move to this 1799 country manor, which, though ostensibly the official mayoral residence, is now used to house visiting dignitaries and host official functions.

Jewish Museum ★ – *1109 Fifth Ave. at 92nd St. 212-423-3200. www.jewishmuseum.org. Open year-round Mon–Thu 11am–5:45pm (Thu until 8pm), Fri 11am–3pm, Sun 10am–5:45pm. Closed Sat & Jewish holidays. $8. 4, 5 or 6 train to 86th St.*
"Culture and Continuity: The Jewish Journey," the two-floor permanent exhibit, traces the evolution of Jewish culture from antiquity to the present.

Museum of Television and Radio ★ – **[M4]** *refers to map on inside front cover. 25 W. 52nd St. between Fifth & Sixth Aves. 212-621-6800. www.mtr.org. Open year-round Tue–Sun noon–6pm (Thu until 8pm). $10. E or V train to Fifth Ave./53rd St.*
Think cable has a lot of offerings? Visitors to this groundbreaking museum can view more than 110,000 radio and television programs and commercials.

Studio Museum in Harlem ★ – *144 W. 125th St. 212-864-4500. www.studiomuseum.org. Open Wed–Fri noon–6pm (Fri until 8pm), weekends 10am–6pm. $5. 2 train to 125th St.*
A major expansion recently added 2,500sq ft of new gallery space to Studio Museum. The museum mounts eight temporary shows a year, working in selections from the permanent collection of more than 1,600 works by prominent artists of African descent.

New York tends to look toward the future, not the past. But history is key to understanding this booming metropolis. The following sites offer glimpses of the Big Apple when it was just a tiny fruit.

City Hall★★

In City Hall Park, bounded by Broadway, Lafayette & Chambers Sts. Visit by guided tour only (see sidebar). N or R train to City Hall.

New York's third city hall, inaugurated in 1812, was designed by Joseph F. Mangin and John McComb Jr., who shared a prize of $350 for their efforts. Atop the graceful cupola is *Justice* with her scales; out front stands a statue of patriot Nathan Hale. The clock was added in 1831. Until 1956 City Hall was half brownstone, not by design but by political penny-pinching. Abraham Lincoln's body lay in state here in April 1865. In the mid-19C, infamous Mayor "Boss" William Tweed made the hall the center of his crime ring, bilking the city out of $30 million. Today City Hall hosts welcoming ceremonies for visiting dignitaries and is the end point of ticker-tape parades—from the first one, held in 1886 to celebrate the dedication of the Statue of Liberty, to the parade for the New York Yankees when they won the World Series in 2000.

Visiting City Hall

City Hall is only open to the public by guided tour. Free one-hour guided tours are held on the second and fourth Fridays of the month. Call early; tours fill up weeks in advance *(212-788-3000)*.

Exterior Highlights – During the 1956 restoration the entire structure was refinished in Alabama limestone.

Interior Highlights – The gallery is ringed by Corinthian columns, which support a coffered dome pierced by a small circular window. The Governor's Room holds a desk used by George Washington.

South Street Seaport Historic District★★

Visitor center at 12-14 Fulton St. 212-748-8600. www.southstseaport.com. Open year-round Mon–Sat 10am–9pm, Sun 11am–8pm. Closed Jan 1, Thanksgiving Day & Dec. 25. 2 or 3 train to Fulton St.

One of New York's leading tourist attractions, South Street Seaport Historic District encompasses an 11-block area fronting the East River, south of the Brooklyn Bridge. The area was the heart of the Port of New York and center of its worldwide shipping activities in the early 19C. Extensive renovation and new construction in the 1980s have transformed the area bounded by John, South, Water, and Beekman streets into a complex of pedestrian malls, museums, restaurants, big chain stores and boutiques. During the summer, open-air concerts draw throngs of visitors to the piers.

Fulton Fish Market

Adjacent to Pier 17. 212-748-8786. Guided tours available on the first & third Wed of every month. This famous wholesale fish market, located in a structure built for the market in 1869, is one of the last outdoor markets in Manhattan and still ranks as the largest in the country. The market comes to life every night from midnight to 8am, when refrigerated trucks unload their fishy goods and chefs and grocers come to pick out the catch of the day. In summer 2004, the market will move to a new facility in the Bronx.

Pier 17 Pavilion★ – You'll find more than 100 shops and restaurants inside this three-story glass and steel structure.

Historic Vessels★ – You can board a barque, a square-rigger, a lightship, a schooner and a tug that are moored along Piers 15 and 16.

Harbor Cruises – Sail New York Harbor aboard the 1885 schooner *Pioneer*. Sponsored by the South Street Seaport museum, cruises depart from Pier 16 *(May–Sept; 2hrs round-trip; 212-748-8786).*

Villard Houses (New York Palace Hotel) ★★

[J] *refers to map on inside front cover. 451-457 Madison Ave. at 51st St. E or V train to Fifth Ave./53rd St.*

In 1881 Henry Villard, a Bavarian immigrant who founded the *New York Evening Post* and the Northern Pacific Railroad, hired the esteemed architectural firm McKim, Mead and White to design a group of six town houses—one for himself and the other five for sale. The outcome was patterned after a 15C Italian palace, with the six four-story structures encircling a U-shaped courtyard. Villard moved in with his family in 1883 but declared bankruptcy shortly afterward and had to sell the complex. It passed from private hands to the New York Archdiocese (St. Patrick's Cathedral is directly across the street) and then, in the 1970s, to Harry Helmsley, a hotel developer. Helmsley wanted to tear down the houses, but the Landmarks Preservation Commission stopped him. So, he built 48 stories on top of the houses instead. The good news is that, as long as you don't look up, the houses appear much as they did when they were built, and some of the sumptuous interiors are preserved.

Urban Center Books

*457 Madison Ave. 212-935-3592.
www.urbancenterbooks.org.* This
friendly little bookstore on the first
floor of the Villard Houses has 9,000
titles on architecture, urbanism and
design. The shop was founded by the
nonprofit Municipal Art Society in
1980 in an effort to foster a more
informed discussion of architecture
and the design arts in New York City—
a goal no doubt informed by the decision to balance a skyscraper on the
Villard Houses' heads.

Interior – Enter through the Madison
Avenue courtyard, particularly pretty
at night, when it is lined with sparkling
white lights. Now part of Le Cirque
2000 restaurant, the Gold Room
shows off a barrel-vaulted ceiling, a
musicians' gallery and lunette paintings by 19C artist John LaFarge.
Adorned with Venetian mosaics, the
great hallway features a sweeping
marble staircase graced with Tiffany
stained-glass windows and a gilt and
marble zodiac clock by Augustus Saint-
Gaudens.

Castle Clinton National Monument★

*Battery Park. 212-344-7220. www.nps.gov/cacl. Open year-round daily 8:30am–5pm.
Closed Dec 25. 4 or 5 train to Bowling Green; 1 or 9 train to South Ferry.*

Its 8ft-thick walls pierced with gun ports, this old fort has had nine lives. Well,
at least five. It was completed in 1811 on an artificial harbor island created to
protect Manhattan from possible attack during the War of 1812. That attack
never happened, so in 1823 the fort was deeded to New York City (and briefly
named after city mayor, Dewitt Clinton) and leased out as a restaurant and
concert hall called Castle Garden.
French general Lafayette was feted here
in 1824, and in 1850 "Swedish nightin-
gale" Jenny Lind made her American
debut on its stage, courtesy of circus
ringleader P.T. Barnum. In 1855 the
fort was returned to state hands and
opened as an immigrant landing depot,

Promenade★★

Meandering from Castle Clinton to
the Staten Island Ferry Terminal, this
walkway offers magnificent
views★★★ of the bay, including the
Statue of Liberty, Ellis Island and
Governors Island.

processing more than eight million new Americans before the Ellis Island station appeared in 1892. In 1870 the harbor between the Castle and the shoreline was filled in and turned into the park you see today. Then, in 1898, the fort was born again as the New York Aquarium, which remained here until 1942 (the aquarium is now at Coney Island). Castle Clinton was designated a national monument in 1950.

Federal Hall National Memorial★

[K] refers to map on inside front cover. 26 Wall St. 212-825-6888. www.nps.gov/feha. Open year-round Mon–Fri 9am–5pm. Closed weekends & major holidays. 2,3, 4 or 5 train to Wall St.

Federal Hall marks the spot of two historic firsts. New York's first city hall was opened here in 1702. Then in 1789, Federal Hall hosted the swearing-in of George Washington as the nation's first president. Alas, that structure was demolished in 1812 and sold as salvage for $425, but its 1842 replacement is sufficiently grand (and Greek) to recall the democratic ideals of the Founding Fathers. A bronze likeness of Washington stands outside on a platform if you need reminding.

Fraunces Tavern Museum★

54 Pearl St. 212-425-1778. www.frauncestavernmuseum. org. Open year-round Tue–Sat 10am–5pm (thu until 7pm). $3. Closed Sun & major holidays. 1 or 9 train to South Ferry; N or R train to Whitehall St.

Fraunces Tavern (originally built in 1719) hosted many events related to the Revolution, including the plotting of the New York Tea Party. An 18-pound cannonball from a British warship tore through its roof in 1775. In the 1780s the building held cabinet offices of the young US government. Damaged in several fires during the 19C, the building was almost entirely reconstructed in 1907. Exhibits here trace the history of early New York and the Revolutionary War.

General Grant National Memorial★

Riverside Dr. at W. 122nd St. 212-666-1640. www.nps.gov/gegr. Open year-round daily 9am–5pm. Closed Jan 1, Thanksgiving Day & Dec 25. 1 or 9 train to 116th St.

"Let us have peace," Ulysses S. Grant wrote to the Republican Party in 1868 when he decided to run for president under its auspices. These words are now engraved above the portico of the white-granite mausoleum, popularly known as Grant's Tomb. A West Point graduate, Grant made his name as Commander of the Union Army during the Civil War, then served two terms in the White House (1869–1877). In 1885, after Grant died of throat cancer, approximately 90,000 people from around the country donated $600,000 to build this Neo-classical memorial in his honor. To answer that old joke, both Grant and his wife, Julia, are buried here.

Morris-Jumel Mansion★

W. 160th St. & Edgecombe Ave. 212-923-8008. www.morrisjumel.org. Open year-round Wed–Sun 10am–4pm. $3. Closed Mon, Tue & major holidays. C train to 163rd St.

This hilltop mansion has stories to tell. Built for British colonel Roger Morris in 1765 as a summer retreat, the house today is Manhattan's oldest residence, containing a wealth of fine antiques and architectural details. A year after Morris abandoned the house in 1775, because his Loyalist sentiments were no longer appreciated in the colonies, George Washington commandeered it during the Battle of Harlem Heights. In 1810 it was acquired by French wine merchant Stephen Jumel, who preferred Napoleonic social circles to New York Society (the bed in the house was a gift from French Emperor Napoleon, who was a friend of the Jumels).

New York Stock Exchange★

[L] *refers to map on inside front cover. 8-18 Broad St. 212-656-5165.
www.nyse.com. 2, 3, 4 or 5 train to Wall St. The stock exchange has been closed
to visitors since Sept. 11, 2001. Call or check Web site for updates.*

This is the place where fortunes are made and broken.
Home of the "Big Board" of
nearly 3,000 publicly traded
companies, the New York
Stock Exchange occupies a
stunning eight-story Greek
Revival building. Its begin-
nings, however, were a bit
more humble: The exchange
was formally established on
May 17, 1792, when 24 brokers
met under a buttonwood
(sycamore) tree outside the
entrance at 20 Wall Street.

Since shortly after the September 11, 2001 attacks, a massive American flag has
stretched across its six 52ft-high Corinthian columns. Behind the columns is a
four-story, glass-curtain wall that allows light to filter into the marble and gilt
trading room.

Trading Places
• NYSE boasts an annual trading volume of $5.5 billion a year.
• NYSE is the world's largest stock exchange.
• The trading area of the NYSE is two-thirds the size of a football field.
• NYSE can process 4,000 orders, quotes and cancels per second.

Theodore Roosevelt Birthplace
National Historic Site★

*28 E. 20th St. 212-260-1616. www.nps.gov/thrb. Open year-round Tue–Sat 9am–5pm. $3.
Closed Sun, Mon & major holidays. 6 train to 23rd Street.*

A born-and-bred New Yorker, Theodore Roosevelt (1858–1919) was not your
average city kid. As a sickly child, he was encouraged to exercise. The advice
stuck, and the outdoors would become Roosevelt's lifelong passion. After
going to college at Harvard, he worked as a rancher in the Dakota Territory,
served as a colonel in the Rough Riders, hunted, collected specimens, and
authored some 30 books. This in addition to being the 26th president of the
United States (1901–09) and the winner of the Nobel Peace Prize in 1906.
Although Roosevelt's true birthplace was demolished in 1916, this Victorian
brownstone was constructed and furnished to look like it did after his death.

World Trade Center Site★

Bounded by Church, Liberty, West & Barclay Sts. www.renewnyc.com. E train to World Trade Center; N or R train to Cortlandt St.

The world's largest commercial complex stood here from 1970 until the morning of September 11, 2001, when two hijacked planes were flown into the Twin Towers, killing more than 2,800 people and bringing the 110-story structures—in which 50,000 people had worked—to the ground. It was the deadliest terrorist attack in US history. Rescue and recovery efforts began immediately, but there were few survivors of what *New Yorker* writer Hendrik Hertzberg called "the catastrophe that turned the foot of Manhattan into the mouth of hell." In all, at least seven buildings were destroyed. Workers carted off 1.5 million tons of steel and debris until the site was clear in May 2002.

In February 2003, "Memory Foundations," a design by the Polish-born architect Daniel Libeskind, was chosen as the blueprint for rebuilding the 16-acre site. In Libeskind's plan, a 1,776ft-tall spire and a cluster of shorter, angular glass buildings encircle two public spaces, the Park of Heroes and the Wedge of Light. Libeskind proposes to leave exposed the slurry walls built around the World Trade Center's foundations because he believes they represent the "durability of democracy."

A formal memorial will be designed by another artist. Construction schedules have not been set, but before a single I-beam is in place there will surely be more wrangling among developers, the lease holder, the public, and the families of the dead, over the future of this tragic space.

Viewing Wall – On a wall erected along Church and Liberty streets, panels trace the history and lay out the future of the site in text, photos and maps. If you peer through the fence you can see the vast moonscape covered with construction equipment.

Sphere – A 15ft-diameter, 22-ton brass sculpture by Fritz Koenig, once the centerpiece of the World Trade Center's plaza, now stands dented and punctured at the entrance to Battery Park *(intersection of Battery Pl. & State St.).*

CHURCHES

Cathedral of St. John the Divine★★

Amsterdam Ave at W. 112th St. 212-316-7540. www.stjohndivine.org. 1 or 9 train to 110th St./Cathedral Pkwy.

This massive stone edifice, the seat of the Episcopal Diocese of New York, is reputedly the largest Gothic cathedral in the world. Strangely, though, it's only two-thirds complete, and there are currently no plans to finish it. The present design, by Boston architect Ralph Adams Cram, incorporates a **Great Rose Window** (it contains 10,000 pieces of glass) overlooking the 601ft-long nave.

Saint Patrick's Cathedral★★

[N] *refers to map on inside front cover. Fifth Ave between 50th & 51st Sts. 212-753-2261. www.ny-archdiocese.org/pastoral. B, D, Q or V train to 47th-50th Sts./Rockefeller Center.*

Saint Patrick's may be the largest Roman Catholic church in the US, but it looks practically quaint amid the skyscrapers of Midtown. When construction began in 1853, people complained that the cathedral was too far out in the country. By the time it was completed in 1879—15 years later than expected—the neighborhood was a fashionable residential quarter. The Gothic Revival-style cathedral, designed by James Renwick, is dedicated to the patron saint of the Irish. The centerpiece of the interior is a 57ft-high bronze canopy, or baldachin.

St. Paul's Chapel★★

Broadway between Fulton & Vesey Sts. 212-602-0800. www.trinitywallstreetorg. Closed Sat & major holidays. 4 train to Fulton St.

Directly across the street from the World Trade Center site amid a grassy fenced-in yard stands this picturesque chapel, which belongs to the Trinity Church Parish *(see below)*. Completed in 1766, the chapel resembles the Church of St. Martin-in-the-Fields in London and is the oldest public building in continuous use in Manhattan. George Washington worshiped here regularly after his inauguration; his pew is in the north aisle.

Trinity Church★★

Broadway & Wall St. 212-602-0800. www.trinitywallstreet.org. 4 train to Wall Street.

No match for the high rises of the Financial District today, this lovely Episcopal church, with its 208ft spire, was the tallest building in New York when it was completed in 1846. The green, shady churchyard is dotted with old tombstones; the most famous marks the grave of former Treasury secretary Alexander Hamilton.

Parks

Far from being a concrete jungle, New York City has plenty of green space—
if you know where to look. From the tiny vest-pocket parks sprinkled
throughout the Village to the 843-acre Central Park, they come in all shapes in
sizes. Some offer bike rentals, hot dog vendors and paddleboats; others just
provide a quiet place to read a book. Take your pick: there are 1,700 to choose
from. Here are some of the best.

Central Park★★★

*Bounded by 59th & 125th Sts. and Central Park West & Fifth Ave. www.centralparknyc.org.
N or R train to Fifth Ave.; A, B, C, 1 or 9 train to 59th St./Columbus Circle.*

Manhattan's playground is justifiably
one of the most famous urban parks in
the world. Not only is it massive—2.5
miles long and a mile across—but it is
rich and varied, offering a multitude of
views; tons of recreational activities;
and plenty of room to stroll, skate,
cycle or just explore. Amazingly, it is
totally man-made. In 1850 newspaper
editor William Cullen Bryant urged the
city government to acquire a "waste

> **Tavern On The Green**
> *West side of the park at 67th St.*
> *212-873-3200. www.tavernonthegreen.
> com.*.The famed tavern is a perfect
> Sunday brunch spot (be sure to
> reserve), with stained-glass windows,
> hand-carved mirrors and glittering
> crystal chandeliers. Weather permit-
> ting, head for the outdoor cafe and
> enjoy the view of the park.

land, ugly and repulsive" north of 42nd Street (the city's northern border at
the time) for use as a park. The city complied, buying what was then a swamp
inhabited by squatters who raised pigs and goats. Calvert Vaux and Frederick
Law Olmsted's naturalistic design was selected, and in 1857 clearing began.
Some 3,000 mostly unemployed Irish workers and 400 horses moved an esti-
mated billion cubic feet of earth over a period of 19 years to make the blueprint green. In the northern part, rocky crags and dense thickets of trees were
made to resemble the landscape of the Adirondack Mountains; in the south
are more pastoral sections of rolling meadows, winding paths and delicate
bridges. Today stately rows of skyscrapers and apartment buildings encircle
the park, but Olmsted's vision remains stunningly intact.

Parks

Best of Central Park

For the **Carousel**★, **Central Park Wildlife Center**★, *and the* **Swedish Cottage Marionette Theatre**, *see Musts for Kids.*

Bethesda Terrace★ – *At 72nd St.* Considered the centerpiece of the park, this lovely sandstone plaza resembles a Spanish courtyard with its arcaded bridge, Minton ceiling tiles, sweeping stairs and central fountain. It adjoins the Mall, a straight wide path lined with handsome elms and sculptures depicting famous writers.

Tips For Visiting Central Park

For information on special events, public programs and recreation facilities, call 212-360-3444. Maps and activity calendars are available at four visitor centers throughout the park *(212-310-6600)*. In-line and ice skates (in season) may be rented at the Wollman Rink *(212-396-1010)*; rent boats and bicycles at Loeb Boathouse *(212-517-2233)*.

Belvedere Castle – *At 79th St. 212-772-0210.* Calvert Vaux built this structure in 1872 as a Victorian folly. Since 1996 its two floors have been home to the **Henry Luce Nature Observatory** *(see Musts for Kids)*, with hands-on exhibits about the city's flora and fauna. Don't miss the tree loft with its papier-mâché reproductions of birds found in Central Park.

Lake – This 22-acre water body, between 71st and 78th streets, is the park's largest (besides the reservoir). Explore it by boat, foot, or gondola. To the west lie the Strawberry Fields and a peace garden honoring the late Beatle John Lennon.

Shakespeare Garden – A rustic four-acre garden on the rocky hillside between Belvedere Castle and the Swedish Cottage is scattered with plaques bearing quotations from the Bard.

Battery Park★

Bordered by Battery Pl. & State St. 4 or 5 train to Bowling Green; 1 or 9 train to South Ferry.

On the southwestern tip of Manhattan, the maze of stone and steel monoliths dominating the Financial District suddenly gives way to a vast expanse of greenery. Strolling along Battery Park's waterfront promenade *(see p58)*, you can enjoy one of the most spectacular panoramas on the Eastern Seaboard. The park gets its name from two forts, East and West Battery, erected offshore to protect the city from British invasion during the War of 1812. In 1870 the harbor between West Battery and the shoreline was filled in and turned into a park. Today it encompasses 21 rolling acres extending from Bowling Green to the junction of the Hudson and East rivers.

Things To See In Battery Park

Sphere – Recovered from the wreckage of the World Trade Center, Fritz Koening's metal sculpture now stands beside an eternal flame.

Castle Clinton National Monument★ – Formerly West Battery. *See Historic Sites.*

Skyscraper Museum – *212-968-1961. www.skyscraper.org.* Exhibits in this brand-new museum in Battery Park City, on the ground floor of the Ritz-Carlton Hotel, chart the rise and rise of New York's skyline.

Bryant Park★

[P] *refers to map on inside front cover. 42nd St. at 6th Ave.*
www.bryantpark.org. B, D, F, Q, V or 7 train to 42nd St.

With its delicate green folding chairs, pebble walkways and London plane trees, this gracious formal park behind the library is Midtown's only large green space. Designated public land since the late 17C, in 1853 and 1854 the site hosted New York's first world's fair, the Crystal Palace Exhibition. The park was named for poet William Cullen Bryant in 1884 (note the 1911 bronze memorial near the library). On summer evenings, free movies are projected on a huge screen in the park *(call 212-512-5700 for schedule)*.

Union Square★

Bounded by E. 14th & E. 17th Sts. and Park Ave. & University Pl. 4, 5, 6, N, R, or L train to 14th St./Union Square.

The greenery is mostly kept out of reach (and alive) behind wrought-iron fences, but walks and benches beneath a canopy of trees make the park a pleasant place to stroll. At the plaza at the southern end, street performers, particularly break-dancers, show off their chops to huge crowds. Initially conceived as a stopover point on the Post Road to Albany, Union Square Park was laid out in 1831. At that point the city was south of the square, but during the 1840s and 1850s residents spread northward and the square became the center of a fashionable neighborhood.

> **Union Square Greenmarket**
>
> *E. 17th to E. 14th Sts., between Park Ave. & University Pl. www.cenyc.org.* From 8am to 6pm on Mondays, Wednesdays, Fridays and Saturdays, Upstate New York's farm bounty comes to this bustling market—a favorite of chefs citywide. Arrive early for the best selection of tubers and herbs, fresh poultry and eggs, dazzling fresh flower arrangements, and wonderful pastries and breads.

Washington Square★

At the south end of Fifth Ave., at the intersection with Waverly Pl. Any train to W. 4th St.

There's not much flora in this park, and the fauna outside of the dog run is mostly human, but New Yorkers flock to this lively square at the heart of Greenwich Village. Originally a marshland and a favorite hunting ground of the early colonists, the site became a potter's field in the 18C (about 1,000 skeletons were unearthed during renovations in the 1960s). Following its transformation into a park in 1826, it spurred the growth of a fashionable residential enclave of redbrick town houses. Today, though, the scene is a bit seedier. New York University's de facto campus green, the park often teems with students, buskers, skateboarders, pamphleteers and pigeon-feeders.

> **Washington Arch★**
>
> Designed by Stanford White in 1892, this white marble Village landmark was built to memorialize George Washington's inauguration as the first US president. The arch measures 30ft across and 70ft high; gracing the sides are two sculptures of Washington, one as a soldier, the other as a civilian.

Neighborhoods

New York is a lively place in part because it is a city of neighborhoods, each with its own character, yet always in flux. From block to block, you never know what you'll come upon. That's why so many visitors leave New York complaining about sore legs: walking is the best way to find out.

Chinatown★★

Bounded by Canal, Mott, Bayard & Pell Sts. N, R or W train to Canal St.; B, D or Q train to Grand St.

Sprawling Chinatown is a veritable city within a city. The narrow streets are lined with colorful shops, and restaurants teem with people, especially on the weekends. The first Chinese to settle in New York came via the western states, where they had worked in the California goldfields or on the transcontinental railroad. The majority were men who had no intention of staying; they merely wished to make their fortunes and return to a comfortable life in China. Ultimately, many formed families or were joined by relatives from back home.

Today Chinatown is one of New York's most densely populated neighborhoods, and it continues to grow past its old boundaries into Little Italy and the formerly Jewish Lower East Side. It is also among the liveliest—scores of restaurants crammed shoulder to shoulder serve Cantonese, Hunan, Mandarin, and Szechuan cuisine late into the night.

Shopping – Canal, Mott, Bayard and Pell streets form the heart of Chinatown, where markets sell everything from duck eggs and mushrooms to jade and ivory carvings, brocade dresses, paper lanterns and tea sets. Always rumbling with trucks, Canal is lined with tiny booths crammed full of knock-off designer goods. Word has it that a secret network of passages and hidden rooms connects some of the stores, allowing proprietors to hide merchandise and move contraband.

Neighborhoods

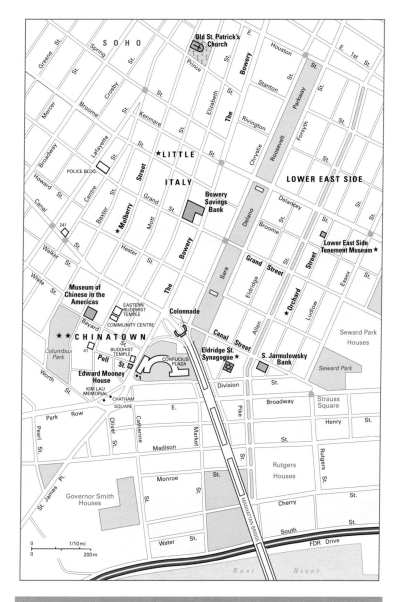

Dim Sum

A visit to Chinatown just isn't complete without a visit to one of its renowned dim sum palaces. Pick from a variety of delicious appetizers, including bao (steamed buns) and harkow (steamed shrimp dumplings). Among your best bets are **Nice Restaurant** at 35 E. Broadway *(212-406-9510)*, which bustles at lunch, and **H.S.F.** at 46 Bowery *(212-374-1319)*, where an illustrated chart will help you identify the 75 offerings.

Greenwich Village★★

Bounded by Spring & 14th Sts., between Greenwich St. & Broadway. A, C, E, F or V train to W. 4th St.; 1 or 2 train to Christopher St.

New York's historic bohemia centers on Washington Square and extends west to the Hudson in a beguiling tangle of gorgeous streets lined with trees and town houses. Starting as an Algonquin Indian settlement called *Sapokanikan*, the site gave rise to a British village in 1696. Artists and intellectuals, including Edgar Allan Poe, began arriving in the 1840s. The trickle turned into a flood in the early 1900s, and the 1960s saw figures such as Bob Dylan putting down roots here. Since then the struggling-artist crowd has moved to the edgier East Village, but Greenwich Village retains a charm all its own, especially west of Sixth Avenue.

What's What In The Village
• **Forbes Galleries**★★ – *See Museums.*
• **Washington Square**★★ – *See Parks.*
• **Bleecker Street**★ – Coffeehouses, record shops and music clubs line this busy commercial strip.
• **Washington Square North**★ – Two blocks of Greek Revival town houses have survived from the 1830s.

SoHo★★

Bounded by Canal & Houston Sts. and Lafayette & Sixth Aves. 1 or 9 train to Prince St.; N or R train to Spring St.

The heart of Manhattan's downtown art and fashion scene has grown increasingly commercial in the past decade, leading some to wonder if it has lost its edge. Perhaps, but it hasn't lost its popularity. Visitors throng here to shop on weekends, popping in and out of shops to browse at sidewalk tables full of handmade purses and jewelry *(see Must Shop)*. The area was settled in 1644 by

former slaves of the Dutch West India Company who were granted land for farms. Dry-goods warehouses were built in the late 19C, some with remarkable cast-iron facades, which looked like carved stone but could be made at a fraction of the cost. Stroll down cobblestone **Greene Street**★ for a look at the district's richest collection of cast-iron structures.

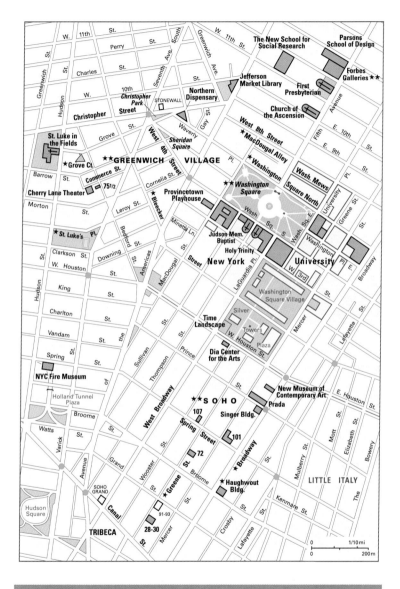

TriBeCa ★

1 or 9 train to Franklin St. www.tribeca.org.

Far less crowded and commercial than its neighbor SoHo, the wedge-shaped district named for its shape and location (TRIangle BElow CAnal) is an intriguing district of warehouses, art spaces, luxury co-ops, and chic restaurants such as **Chanterelle**, **Nobu** and Robert De Niro's **Tribeca Grill**.

Upper East Side★★

From 59th St. to 97th St., between Central Park & the East River. N or R train to Fifth Ave.; 6 train to any station between 59th & 97th Sts.

Although Millionaires' Row is now Museum Mile, the Upper East Side is still the wealthiest neighborhood in the city. In the late 19C, rich industrialists including Andrew Carnegie and Henry Clay Frick began building mansions on the large lots along Fifth Avenue abutting the park. The ladies who lunch followed on their heels, moving into then-new luxury apartment buildings along Park Avenue and town houses on the side streets. Today **Fifth Avenue**★★ remains the neighborhood's most impressive thoroughfare; **Madison Avenue**★ is chock-a-block with exclusive shops and art galleries; and **Park Avenue**★ is an elegant residential boulevard.

Museum Mile *(for descriptions of individual sites, see Museums)*	
Frick Collection★★★	Metropolitan Museum of Art★★★
Guggenheim Museum★★	Whitney Museum★★
Cooper-Hewitt National Design Museum★	Asia Society★
Jewish Museum★	Museum of the City of New York★
Neue Galerie★	

Upper West Side★★

From Columbus Circle to W. 125th St. between Central Park & the Hudson River. Any train to Columbus Circle/59th St.; 1 or 9 train north to 102nd St.

Great cultural institutions and great food are what you can expect from the Upper West Side, along with tidy rows of restored brownstones and stunning apartment buildings bordering Central Park. Development has been relatively recent. In the late 19C much of the area was still populated by stray goats. When New York's first luxury apartment house was erected on West 72nd Street and Central Park West in 1884, it was considered so far away from the heart of the city that it was dubbed the **Dakota** (Henry Hardenbergh's Gothic pile has since become famous as the site of John Lennon's murder). Noel Coward, Babe Ruth, Dustin Hoffman, and Jerry Seinfeld are just some of the famous residents who have called this neighborhood home over the years.

Upper West Side Highlights
• **American Museum of Natural History**★★★ – *Central Park West between 77nd & 81st Sts. See Museums.*
• **New-York Historical Society**★★ – *2 W. 77th St. at Central Park West See Museums.*
• **Cathedral of St. John the Divine**★ – *Amsterdam Ave. at W. 112th St. See Landmarks*
• **Lincoln Center**★★ – *Broadway between 62nd & 67th Sts. See Performing Arts.*

Chelsea★

West of Sixth Ave. between 14th & 30th Sts. 1, 9 or F, V train to 23rd St.

Beautifully refurbished brownstones and a thriving arts scene have made Chelsea a very desirable address in recent years, especially in the gay community. It was named after the London neighborhood of the same name in the mid-18C but most of its housing stock dates to the 19C, when it was laid out. Today Chelsea is *the* place in New York for gallery hopping. Pick up the local listings to see what's hot.

Chelsea Piers – *Along West Side Hwy. between 17th & 23rd Sts. www.chelseapiers.com.* The city's premier recreational venue, the 30-acre sports village offers everything from in-line skating to sailing. There's even a golf course and a rock-climbing wall.

26th Street Flea Market – One of the city's largest outdoor markets takes place every Saturday and Sunday, when scores of amateur dealers gather in a vacant lot between 26th and 27th streets on the Avenue of the Americas to display an amazing collection of odds and ends, with a few antiques thrown in.

Chelsea Galleries

Galleries are generally open Tue–Sat from 10am to 5pm or 11am to 5pm or 6pm (later on opening nights).

Barbara Gladstone Gallery – *515 W. 24th St. 212-206-9300. www.gladstonegallery.com.* This SoHo emigré shows work by top video and conceptual artists.

Dia: Chelsea – *548 W. 22nd St. 212-989-5566. www.diachelsea.org.* Mounts long-term, site-specific work by up-and-coming artists.

Greene Naftali – *526 W. 26th St. 212-463-7770.* Showcases contemporary international art.

Matthew Marks – *522 W. 22nd St. & 523 W. 23rd St. 212-243-0200. www.matthewmarks.com.* Presents big names in contemporary painting, sculpture and photography.

Paula Cooper Gallery – *534 W. 21st St. 212-255-1105.* Has long been a champion of conceptual and minimalist art.

Harlem★

Above 106th St. in the east and 110th & 125th Sts. in the west. Any train to 125th St.

The architectural treasures alone warrant a visit to this incredibly diverse neighborhood, which is actually two Harlems. East of Fifth Avenue and north of 106th Street lies East Harlem, or the *barrio*, with its distinctive Puerto Rican flavor; west of Fifth Avenue is central Harlem, which is mostly African American. The neighborhood dates back to 1658 but was mostly rural until the railroad and elevated trains linked it to the rest of the city in the 19C. By the early 1890s it was one of New York's most fashionable enclaves. The Harlem Renaissance came in the 1920s when black musicians (Count Basie, Duke Ellington) and writers (Zora Neale Hurston, Langston Hughes) electrified the world with their originality. Recent investment has brought new life into some of the once-grand residences. Former president Bill Clinton, for instance, established his offices on 125th Street, and the famous Apollo Theater just completed a $12 million face lift.

Studio Museum in Harlem★ – *144 W. 125th St. See Museums.*

Tips For Visiting

Because the neighborhood is very large, we recommend taking a tour or at least getting a detailed map. The **Harlem Tourist Center and Harlem Gift Shop** offers both *(2224 Frederick Douglass Blvd. between 119th & 120th Sts. 212-749-5700. www.hatt.org).*

Sylvia's

328 Lenox between 126th & 127th Sts. 212-996-0660. The most celebrated soul-food restaurant in Harlem, Sylvia's is also a hub of the Harlem community. Order the delicious greens, candied yams and fried chicken. For a special treat, come for the Sunday gospel brunch.

Little Italy★

See map p 69. Bounded by Canal, Lafayette & Houston Sts., and the Bowery. B, D or Q train to Grand St.

Little Italy is one of the most wonderful corners of the city, with cafes for cappuccino and cannoli; grocery stores full of fresh pasta, salamis, olives and cheeses; and friendly and inexpensive red-sauce joints. The area took on its Italian character between the 1880s and the 1920s, when thousands of migrants left epidemics and poverty in Sicily and Southern Italy to come to the US. Mostly arriving through Ellis Island, they formed one of the city's tightest-knit communities. Though today the neighborhood is being pinched by burgeoning Chinatown to the east and SoHo to the west, a sense of place still prevails.

Mulberry Street★ – Sometimes called the Via San Gennaro, Mulberry Street is Little Italy's heart. The thoroughfare becomes a vast al fresco restaurant during the popular **Feast of San Gennaro** in mid-September.

Eating in Little Italy

For great desserts and espresso, head to **Ferrara Cafe and Bakery** on Grand Street *(no. 195; 212-226-6150)*. **Caffè Napoli** *(191 Hester St.; 212-226-8705)* and **Caffè Roma** *(385 Broome St.; 212-226-8413)* are also good bets. **Puglia's** *(189 Hester St.; 212-966-6006)* is known for its generous portions of veal parmigiana and its singing waiters. **Le Mela** *(167 Mulberry St.; 212-431-9493)* doesn't have a menu, but the food is always delicious, and deliciously cheap. Or try one of the neighborhood's famous seafood restaurants. **Vincent's Clam Bar** *(119 Mott St.; 212-226-8133)* is a true neighborhood institution.

Don't be fooled by its cosmopolitan air—New York City loves to kid around. A city of parents, it teems with fun activities for families. Here's a roundup of some of our favorites.

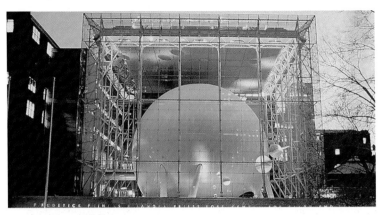

American Museum of Natural History★★★

Central Park West between 77th & 81st Sts. 212-769-5100. www.amnh.org. Open year-round daily 10am–5:45pm (Rose Center open until 8:45pm). $12 (includes admission to Rose Center exhibits). Closed Thanksgiving Day & Dec 25. B, C train to 81st St. or 1, 9 train to 79th St.

There's plenty of awesome stuff here to keep kids mesmerized for hours. Dinosaurs are a good place to start. Check out the huge barosaurus skeleton in Theodore Roosevelt Memorial Hall, then go up to the six fossil halls on the fourth floor—the museum has the largest collection of fossil vertebrates in the world. The Hall of Biodiversity simulates the sights and sounds of an African rain forest, and the new Hall of Ocean Life is an immersion experience. Don't forget the **Rose Center for Earth and Space★★**. First-floor exhibits on the blue planet and its place in the universe are high-tech marvels; tip back in your comfy chair and let Tom Hanks introduce you to astronomical wonders like superclusters and nebulae.

Bronx Zoo★★★

Fordham Rd. & Bronx River Pkwy. 718-367-1010. www.wcs.org. Open Apr–Oct Mon–Fri, 10am–5pm. Rest of the year daily 10am–4:30pm. $11 adults, $8 children (ages 2–12). 2 train to Pelham Pkwy.

The country's largest urban zoo is set in a woodland park that's so pretty you might forget that just around the corner you could meet a giraffe or an ostrich. From elegant ibex to goofy gibbons, the animals here enjoy homes that mirror their natural habitats as much as possible, thanks to the Wildlife Conservation Society, which runs the place. The new exhibit, **Tiger Mountain**, lets you see eye to eye with these Siberian cats. A **Children's Zoo** *($3)* houses more than 500 animals and features a fun prairie-dog exhibit, a rope spider web and a farmyard where kids can feed goats, chickens and the like.

Central Park★★★ for Kids

Bounded by 59th St & 125th St., Central Park West & Fifth Ave. 212-360-3444. www.centralparknyc.org., N or R train to Fifth Ave.; A, B, C, 1 or 9 train to 59th St./ Columbus Circle.

Besides offering plenty of space for sports and strolls, Central Park has attractions that appeal to kids of all ages.

Carousel★ – *At 64th St. 212-879-0244. Open May–Oct daily 10am–6pm. Rest of the year weekends only 10am–4:30pm.* This 1908 model incorporates 58 hand-carved, hand-painted horses—some life size! A New York tradition.

Central Park Wildlife Center★ – *212-439-6500. Open Apr–Oct Mon–Fri 10am–5pm. Rest of the year daily 10am–4:30pm. $6 adults, $1 children (ages 3–12).* Animals in this 5.5-acre zoo have space to roam in natural settings. Kids can pet and feed domestic animals at the **Children's Zoo**. Be sure to see the Delacorte clock over the entrance arch, with its moving bronze animal figures holding musical instruments.

Belvedere Castle – *At 79th St. 212-772-0210. Open Apr–Oct Tue–Sun 10am–4pm. Rest of the year closes at 5pm.* The **Henry Luce Nature Observatory** features kid-friendly hands-on exhibits about the city's flora and fauna.

Charles A. Dana Discovery Center – *212-860-1370. Open year-round Tue–Sat 10am–5pm.* Perched on the shore of the Harlem Meer ("meer" is Dutch for lake) near 110th Street, the center sponsors exhibits and family programs. Rent a pole for catch-and-release fishing on the meer.

Swedish Cottage Marionette Theatre – *Reservations required; 212-988-9093. Shows Tue–Fri 10:30am & noon, Sat 1pm. $6 adults, $5 children.* Original puppet shows, many drawn from fairy tales, are staged daily at this charming 1876 Swedish schoolhouse.

Empire State Building★★★

*Fifth Ave. & 34th St. 212-736-3100. www.esbnyc.com.
Open year-round daily 9:30am–midnight, reduced
hours Jan 1, Dec 24 & 25. $11 adults, $10 ages 12–17, $6
ages 6–11. Any train to 34th St.*

Kids love a trip to the top of this 102-story Art
Deco landmark, where they can get dizzying
views of New York City and its neighboring
states. High-speed elevators zip up to the 86th
floor, which has both a glass-enclosed area and
spacious outdoor promenades on all four sides
of the building. High-powered binoculars let you
zoom in close on your favorite sites *(for more
information, see Landmarks).*

Statue of Liberty★★★

*Liberty Island. 212-363-3200. www.nps.gov/stli. Only
the grounds are currently open. Closed Dec 25. For
more information, see Landmarks.*

After years of seeing her on key chains and
postcards, it's mind-bending to finally be up
close and personal with Lady Liberty. There's a
museum in the pedestal, but it's hard to stay
inside with such amazing views outside! Cork-
screw stairs lead to the crown. As of mid-2003,
the statue was closed for security reasons, but
you can still appreciate her from the grounds or
from the Staten Island Ferry.

Lower East Side Tenement Museum★

*90 and 97 Orchard St. 212-431-0233. www.tenement.org. Visitor center open daily 11am–
5pm, tenement building open Tue–Fri 1pm–4pm, weekends 11am–4:30pm; Confino Family
Apt open weekends only noon–3pm. Ticket prices vary according to tour. F train to
Delancey St.*

One **"living history" tour** *(Sat & Sun at 1, 2, & 3pm)* here is especially geared
for kids. Never breaking character, a guide playing Victoria Confino, a turn-of-
the-20C teenager, will show you her apartment and relate in witty detail how
work was parceled out, how marriages were arranged and how much monthly
rent her family paid for the tiny space—$15, including coal. A must for kids
who've never lived in a big city.

Children's Museum of Manhattan

*212 W. 83rd St. (between Broadway & Amsterdam Ave.). 212-721-1234. www.cmom.org.
Open Tue–Sun 10am–5pm. Closed Mon, Tue (except in summer) & major holidays. $6
(adults & children). 1 or 2 train to 79th St.*

Kids can spend many happy hours at Manhattan's only museum geared for
children. Five floors of hands-on exhibits explore the environment, forensic
science and much more.

Coney Island

*1015 Surf Ave., Brooklyn. 718-266-1234.
www.coneyislandusa.com. F, Q or W train to
Stillwell Ave./Coney Island.*

New York's beachfront amusement park
is a little seedy but tons of fun. Take a stom-
ach-dropping ride on the **Cyclone**, a 1927
wood-framed rollercoaster, ride the gigantic Ferris wheel or catch a circus
sideshow. A stroll along the wood-plank boardwalk that skirts the beach is a
Coney Island tradition, as is a Coney Island hot dog from Nathan's.

New York Aquarium★★

*W. 8th St. & Surf Ave. 718-265-3474. www.nyaquarium.com. Open Apr–May & Sept–
Oct, Mon–Fri 10am–5pm; May–Sept until 6pm. $11 adults, $7 children (ages 2–12).* Just
off the Coney Island boardwalk, check out the aquarium, where whales, seals, seal
lions, dolphins, and Pacific walrus glide around in large outdoor pools. Inside you'll
find a penguin colony and a 90,000-gallon shark tank *(see Boroughs/Brooklyn)*.

Intrepid Sea-Air-Space Museum

*Pier 86 at W. 46th St. & 12th Ave. 212-245-0072.
www.intrepidmuseum.org. Open Apr–Sept daily 10am–
5pm (weekends until 7pm). Closed Mon Oct–Mar, Jan 1,
Thanksgiving Day & Dec 25. $14 adults, $10 ages 12-17, $7
ages 6-11, $2 ages 2-5.*

Berthed at a pier in the Hudson River is the 1943
aircraft carrier USS *Intrepid*. With a length of
898ft and a weight of 42,000 tons, the carrier is a veritable city, providing its
3,500-member crew with everything from a haircut to an ice-cream sundae.

Sony Wonder Lab

*In Sony Plaza, 56th St. between Madison & Fifth Aves. 212-833-8100. www.wondertechlab.
sony.com. Open year-round Tue–Wed Fri–Sat, 10am–6pm, Sun noon–6pm. Closed Mon &
major holidays. E or V train to Fifth Ave./53rd St.*

Interactive exhibits at this futuristic play space will dazzle even the most tech-
savvy kid. Parents take note: If this is one of your child's must-sees, reserve at
least a week ahead.

You can hardly think of New York City without thinking of Broadway shows. And Off-Broadway shows . . . and Off-Off Broadway shows. As the undisputed arts capital of the US, New York offers entertainment for nearly every taste and budget. Here's a list of some of the most popular options in the city, but it's by no means comprehensive. *For daily schedules and critics' picks, consult the publications listed in Practical Information.*

Broadway★★

The Broadway Line: 212-302-4111. www.livebroadway.com.

They say the neon lights are bright on Broadway—and rightly so. "The Great White Way" is synonymous with the country's best and most popular theater productions. Of course, this street isn't the only one lined with theaters; it merely forms the spine of the **Theater District**, which extends roughly between 40th and 53rd streets from 6th to 8th avenues. Crowd-pleasing musicals abound, with some of the best hoofers burning up the boards and bringing down the house in shows like *42nd Street, Chicago,* and *The Producers.* Movie stars and pop-music legends will often open shows that run for years with rotating casts—some better than the originals.

TKTS

Waiting till the last minute doesn't always mean paying top dollar, especially when it comes to theater tickets. If you're flexible with what you want to see, you can save 25 to 50 percent on tickets at TKTS. You can buy tickets for same-day evening performances and matinees at the **Times Square booth** *(Broadway & 47th St.; tickets for evening shows go on sale at 3pm Mon–Sat)* or at the **South Street Seaport booth** *(corner of John & Front Sts.; opens at 11am).* The downtown location also sells tickets for matinees a day in advance. Marquees at both locations indicate which shows have tickets; availability changes hourly. For the best selection, arrive early, though sometimes tickets are released to TKTS just before the 8pm curtain. *Cash and traveler's checks only.*

Lincoln Center★★

Broadway between 62nd & 67th Sts. Tickets: 212-721-6500. Tours: 212-875-5350. www.lincolncenter.org.

Devoted to drama, music and dance, Lincoln Center for the Performing Arts is a 16-acre complex comprising five major theater and concert buildings, a library, a band shell and two outdoor plazas. Visually, the space is stunning, with sleek rectangular buildings of glass and Italian travertine marble arranged around a central fountain. The centerpiece is the **Metropolitan Opera House**, with its 10-story colonnade. Although guided tours are available daily, the best way to appreciate

92nd Street Y—The Other Side Of The Park
1395 Lexington Ave. at 92nd St. 212-415-5500. www.92y.org.
No ordinary YMCA, this Y has been called "the quintessential New York institution" by the *New York Times*. It was founded in 1874 and has grown into one of the city's best-loved cultural centers, presenting world-class concerts of classical, folk and cabaret music, lyric theater and jazz, and readings by eminent authors.

Lincoln Center is to attend a performance. The regular season lasts from September through May; the summer season is filled with festivals and special events, including Lincoln Center Out of Doors, Midsummer Night Swing, Mostly Mozart, and the Lincoln Center Festival.

Resident Companies

Jazz at Lincoln Center – *212-258-9800. www.jazzatlincolncenter.org.* The Lincoln Center Jazz Orchestra performs under the direction of Wynton Marsalis. The orchestra's new home fronting Central Park is expected to open in fall 2004.

Metropolitan Opera – *212-362-6000. www.metopera.org.* The world-renowned company performs in the 3,788-seat opera house.

New York City Ballet – *212-870-5570. www.nycballet.com.* Performs in the 2,792-seat New York State Theater, designed by Philip Johnson.

New York City Opera – *212-870-5630. www.nycopera.org.* Also performs in the New York State Theater.

New York Philharmonic – *212-875-5656. www.newyorkphilharmonic.org.* New York's resident symphony performs in 2,742-seat Avery Fisher Hall, though plans are afoot to move back to Carnegie Hall for the 2004–2005 season.

The Rockettes

. . . 5-6-7-8. The world's finest precision dance team began as the Missouri Rockettes in St. Louis in 1925, and they've been the star attraction at Radio City Music Hall since opening night, December 27, 1932. Today the annual Radio City Christmas Spectacular, with its cast of 150 leggy dancers, is a dazzling New York holiday tradition.

Radio City Music Hall★★

[Q] *refers to map on inside front cover. 1270 Sixth Ave. Tickets: 212-307-7171. Tours: 212-632-4041. www.radiocity.com.*

A treasured New York landmark, this Art Deco performance palace is a spectacular place to see a show—particularly the resident Rockettes, whose kick-line spectaculars are as mesmerizing as the place itself. Radio City opened its doors in 1932 and began by presenting the best vaudeville acts and silent pictures of its day. The 5,882-seat theater has since been the site of some fantastic live performances (everyone from Frank Sinatra to Björk has graced its stage). Its proscenium arch rises six stories.

• **State-of-the-art stage** allows musicians in the orchestra and organists at the two electric Wurlitzers to be whisked away behind the walls or below the floor during performances—without missing a note!

Brooklyn Academy of Music★

30 Lafayette Ave., Brooklyn. 718-636-4100. www.bam.org.

Widely regarded as New York's premier venue for avant-garde performance, BAM hosts live music, dance and theater in two historic buildings. The elegant 1,100-seat opera house has hosted everyone from Enrico Caruso to Laurie Anderson. The 900-seat Harvey Theater, a stripped-down jewel box, is home to the Brooklyn Philharmonic Orchestra and recently hosted plays directed by Sam Mendes and Ingmar Bergman.

Carnegie Hall★

154 W. 57th St. at 7th Ave. Call for schedule of public tours. 212-247-7800. www.carnegiehall.org.

With its fine acoustics, majestic Carnegie Hall is one of the world's most prestigious concert venues. Named after steel magnate Andrew Carnegie, the Italian Renaissance structure opened in 1891 with Tchaikovsky's American conducting debut. Since then its stage has hosted luminaries from Gustav Mahler to Bob Dylan. Carnegie Hall has three performance spaces: the main 2,804-seat auditorium; the 268-seat **Weill Recital Hall**, which resembles a Belle Epoque salon; and the high-tech **Zankel Hall**, with 650 seats—and a museum.

Apollo Theater

253 W. 125th St. Tickets: 212-531-5303. Event information: 212-531-5301. Tours: 212-531-5337. www.apollotheater.com.

This world-famous Harlem theater has been a hotbed of African-American music and entertainment since 1934. Wednesday night is Amateur Night—"where stars are born and legends are made." Who knows? You might see the debut of the next Ella Fitzgerald, James Brown, Michael Jackson, or Lauryn Hill—all of whom launched their careers here. A major renovation of the theater was completed in 2003.

City Center

130 W. 55th St. 212-581-1212. www.citycenter.org. Closed in summer.

After being threatened with demolition in the 1940s, this 1924 Shriner's temple reopened as a concert hall with ticket prices topping out at $2. Since 1994 the popular Encore Series has brought recognition to rarely heard works of American musical theater. City Center's best-known resident companies are the **Alvin Ailey American Dance Theater** *(www.alvinailey.org)* and the **American Ballet Theatre** *(www.abt.org)*.

Off-Broadway Theater

www.offbroadway.com.

There are 150 spaces across the city that qualify as Off-Broadway theaters. While many of them lie outside the Theater District, the designation indicates more than their location. Off-Broadway tickets cost less than those to Broadway shows. Theaters are also smaller (100–500 seats), and performances more intimate. Some shows, like *Stomp* and *Blue Man Group*, remain on Off-Broadway for years. Others *(Urinetown, Rent, Proof, A Chorus Line)* start Off-Broadway and move to Broadway once they become bona fide hits.

Off-Off Broadway

If Off-Broadway doesn't get you far enough away from the Great White Way, consider going Off-Off. Performances can be hit or miss, but the ticket price (usually less than $20) justifies a little risk taking. See the *Village Voice* for reviews.

Famous Off-Broadway Companies & Theaters *(all are based downtown)*:

• Avant-garde **Wooster Group** *(212-966-3651; www.thewoostergroup.org)*

• Progressive **Public Theater** *(212-239-6200; www.publictheater.org)*

• **Theater for a New Audience** *(212-229-2819; www.tfana.org)*

Don't get stressed if you can't see everything on your trip to New York. That's just what a New Yorker would do. Instead, try to relax and have fun, mixing up museum visits with simple pleasures. Here are some places to start.

Times Square★★

Visitor Center at 1560 Broadway between 46th & 47th Sts. 212-768-1560.
1, 2, 3, 7, 9, N or R train to Times Square.

Packed with people day and night—night is a relative term, as it never gets dark—Times Square is the blazing heart of New York, a sensory burst of gigantic neon advertisements and electronic tickers, Jumbotrons, traffic, crowds and vendors. The newly renovated (some say sanitized) district stretches along Broadway between 40th and 47th streets and overflows into the side streets, which host dozens of Broadway theaters *(see Performing Arts)*. Times Square is especially festive at night, when after-theater audiences pour out into the streets to enjoy its bright lights and carnivalesque atmosphere. Don't expect to find any "old" New York here—with its corporate logos and international crowds, the area is now more than ever the crossroads of the world.

Staten Island Ferry★

718-812-2628. siferry.com. Year-round daily 24hrs/day every 30min (hourly after 11pm).
$3/car (on foot, free). 1 or 9 train to South Ferry.

For a quick, dazzling tour of New York Harbor, hop aboard the Staten Island Ferry, a free commuter line *(see Boroughs/Staten Island)*.

Anchors Aweigh!
When it comes to sightseeing, it's time to think outside the grid. To learn the legends and lore of the city, consider taking a **boat tour**, one of the most pleasant ways to get to know New York. A trip may be as short as 30 minutes or as long as 4 hours. Most tours have commentary; some include lunch or dinner. All offer panoramic views and fresh river air. One of the most popular choices is the tour offered by the **Circle Line** *(212-563-3200; circleline.com)*—a full loop around Manhattan narrated by funny, informative guides. The three other lines are **NY Waterway** *(800-533-3779; nywaterway.com)*, **Spirit Cruises** *(212-727-2789; www.spiritcruises.com)* and **World Yacht Dinner Cruises** *(212-630-8100; worldyacht.com)*. Boats leave from South Street Seaport and from piers along Manhattan's West Side.

Big Apple Greeters

212-869-8159. bigapplegreeter.org.

Think all New Yorkers are surly to visitors? Think again. More than 400 residents are on call to give free, specialized tours to out-of-towners. That's right—the service matches tour guides to your needs, time constraints and language requirements. How's that for big-city hospitality?

Carriage Rides in Central Park

*59th St., between Fifth & Sixth Aves. 212-246-0520. N or R train to Fifth Ave.;
A, B, C, 1, or 9 train to 59th St./Columbus Circle.*

Horse-drawn carriages have been a fixture in Central Park since the Victorian era. This old-fashioned mode of transport remains one of the most romantic and popular ways to see Central Park, even (or especially!) during the winter months, when drivers will give you a blanket to snuggle up in.

Grand Central on the Half Shell

*Grand Central Terminal, lower level. 212-490-6650. www.oysterbarny.com.
S, 4, 5, 6 or 7 train to Grand Central.*

Sure, its vaulted ceiling is magnificent (the tiles were designed by Rafael Gustavino), but **Grand Central Oyster Bar** doesn't coast on atmosphere. New Yorkers come here for some of the best fresh seafood in the city. Settle in at the counter and order oysters Rockefeller and clam chowder—it's a tradition—or have a full meal in the restaurant. The steady flow of diners makes for great people-watching.

Madame Tussaud's

*234 W. 42nd St. 212-512-9600. www.madame-tussauds.com. Open daily 10am–6pm
(Fri–Sat until 8pm). $22. 1, 2, 3, 7, 9, N or R train to Times Square.*

If a picture's worth a thousand words, than how many is a wax model worth? Judge for yourself at this wildly popular "museum," named after a woman who made death masks from the guillotined heads of French Revolutionary figures. More than 200 popular and historical personalities come eerily to life in galleries that show them off, warts and all (when they say realistic, they mean it!).

Museum Happy Hour

Would you like a martini with that Matisse? Thought so. Several of the city's best museums—including the **Cooper-Hewitt National Design Museum**, the **Frick**, the **Guggenheim**, the **Met**, and the **Whitney**—keep their doors (and their cafes) open until 9pm on Friday nights, offering free admission after 6pm. It's a great way to kick off a weekend. *For hours & locations, see Museums.*

Rainbow Room★

30 Rockefeller Plaza. 212-632-5000. www.cipriani.com. B, D, F, Q or V train to 47th–50th St./Rockefeller Center.

It would be difficult to find a spot more glamorous, more quintessentially New York, than the 65th floor of the Art Deco GE Building. The place for a cocktail with a view is the Rainbow Grill *(open 5pm–midnight; weekends till 1am; jackets required)*. If you want to pull out all the stops, spend a romantic evening at the Rainbow Room *(open Fri 7pm–1am; black tie optional, dark suit required)*. Here you can have dinner and dance cheek-to-cheek on the revolving dance floor, with all of glittering Manhattan as a backdrop and a live orchestra playing the sound track. For dancing only, arrive after 10pm.

Lights, Camera, Action!

You've seen them on TV—people just like you sitting in the studio audiences of your favorite programs, hooting and hollering on cue. If that's what you're after, try to get tickets to a taping. Though most tickets are spoken for months or even years in advance, you may be able to get stand-by tickets if you're willing to call at a specific time or wait in line. Here's how to get information about some of the shows:

The Late Show with David Letterman – 212-247-6497 or www.cbs.com.

NBC Studio show tickets (including *The Caroline Rhea Show, Last Call with Carson Daly, Late Night with Conan O'Brien,* and *Saturday Night Live*) – 212-664-3056 or www.nbc.com.

Good Morning America – 212-580-5176 or www.abcnews.com.

Live with Regis and Kelly – 212-456-3537 or http://tvplex.go.com/buenavista/ livewithregis.

If all else fails, you can jostle for a spot on camera outside the street-level **Today Show** studio *(30 Rockefeller Plaza between Fifth & Sixth Aves.; Mon–Fri 7am–10am; www.nbc.com)*, or take a **guided tour of NBC studios** *(see Skyscrapers/GE Building)*.

Yankee Stadium Tour

*161st St. & River Ave., the Bronx. 718-579-4531. www.newyork.yankees.mlb.com.
4 train to 161st St.*

Of course, the best way to appreciate the Bronx Bombers is to watch the
26-time world champions in action *(for tickets, call 212-307-1212)*. But for
the skinny on the team and its storied career, a behind-the-scenes tour of
the "house that Babe Ruth built"—the 1923 stadium that has hosted some of
the most dramatic moments in baseball—can't be beat. You get to see the
dugout, the press box, the clubhouse and Monument Park, where bronze
plaques commemorate pinstripe legends Lou Gehrig, Joe DiMaggio, Mickey
Mantle and others.

Seasonal New York

As the proverb goes, for everything there is a season, and that is certainly true in New
York. Even if fall and spring offer the best chance of nice weather, summer and winter
have lots of fun traditions as well. Here are a few.

Winter – Under the watchful gaze of *Prometheus*, caught stealing fire from the gods,
is the center of a winter wonderland—**Rockefeller Center's sunken skating rink** *(212-
332-7654)*. It's cozy—okay, tiny—but taking a turn on the ice in such a splendid setting
is unforgettable. If you need more room to execute your Hamill Camel, head uptown
to Central Park's tree-framed **Wollman Rink**, near Columbus Circle *(212-439-6900; ww
w.wollmanskatingrink.com)*. Skate rentals are available in both places.

Another holiday tradition: Check out the **window displays** at **Macy's** *(34th St. & Sixth
Ave.)* and **Saks Fifth Avenue** *(Fifth Ave. & 49th St.)*. If you're at Saks, be sure to mosey
across the street to see the nine-story **Christmas tree** ablaze with tiny lights in
Rockefeller Plaza.

Summer – July and August can be hot and sticky, and many New Yorkers flee the city.
Well, that's their prerogative, but they're missing out on a great civic tradition: **free
performances**, offered by some of the Big Apple's most renowned theatrical troupes
and music groups. The **Metropolitan Opera**, the **New York Philharmonic** and the
Public Theater all offer freebies in New York's parks. **SummerStage** in Central Park
hosts some terrific performers as well. *For more information, see Calendar of Events
or check local listings.*

Fashion victims unite! No matter if you have champagne tastes and a beer budget—from bargain-laden Orchard Street to the new Crystal District on Madison Avenue, there's something to suit every wallet in the shopping mecca of New York City.

Fifth Avenue★★★

Upscale boutiques and department stores line world-famous Fifth Avenue between 34th and 57th streets. Even if you don't step foot inside a single one, their elaborate window displays turn a simple stroll into a dazzling adventure.

Fifth Avenue Roll Call

- **Bergdorf Goodman** – *Between 57th and 58th Sts. 212-753-7300. www.bergdorfgoodman.com.* Understated elegance has been the key to the store's lasting appeal among Upper East Side "ladies who lunch" and the men who love them.

- **Cartier** – *At 52nd St. 212-753-0111. www.cartier.com.* The French jewelry firm bought this Renaissance-style palazzo in 1917.

- **FAO Schwarz** – *767 Fifth Ave. at 58th St. 212-644-9400. www.fao.com.* Kids of all ages adore this world-famous toy store, founded by German immigrant Frederick August Otto Schwarz in 1862.

- **Lord & Taylor** – *At 37th St. 212-391-3344. www.maycompany.com.* This re-freshingly old-fashioned department store seems impervious to flashy marketing campaigns.

- **Rockefeller Center** – *47th–50th Sts.* Purchase anything from books in Japanese to to Italian leather in the shops lining these plazas and underground concourses.

- **Saks Fifth Avenue** – *At 49th St. 212-753-4000. www.saks.com.* Upper floors at Saks' flagship feature haute-couture boutiques with plenty of clerks on call.

- **Tiffany & Co.** – *727 Fifth Ave. 212-755-8000. www.tiffany.com.* For silver and pearls especially, Tiffany's is still the crème de la crème.

Christmas Windows

For New York's department stores, gearing up for Christmas mean keeping up a long-held tradition of transforming their windows into magical scenes full of moving fig-ures, music and twinkling lights. **Lord & Taylor** *(37th St. & Fifth Ave.)* often has the best displays, in part because the window platforms are on hydraulic lifts (the space used to be an automobile showroom). Come mid-November, a false floor is put in to hold the Thanksgiving displays at street level while designers toil away on the Christmas windows in the basement. When they're ready, the false floor comes out, a button is pressed and—voila!—elaborate displays appear.

Elegant windows at **Saks Fifth Avenue** *(49th St. & Fifth Ave.)* often draw from classic fairy tales. Arrive early to avoid long lines, and afterward, treat yourself to a thick hot chocolate at **Maison du Chocolat** at 30 Rockefeller Center *(49th St. between Fifth & Sixth Aves.; 212 265-9404; www.lamaisonduchocolat.com).* C'est magnifique!

Diamond and Jewelry Way★★

47th St. between Fifth & Sixth Aves. 212-302-5739. www.diamonddistrict.org.
This 750ft block is home to nearly 90 percent of the diamond wholesale trade in the US. Listen closely, and even on the sidewalk you may hear cut, carat, color and clarity—the four "C"s—discussed in a bewildering variety of languages. Most deals, however, are conducted inside these glittering emporia, either in upper-floor dealers' booths or in backrooms. Feel free to browse the heavily monitored showrooms.

Times Square★★

At 42nd St., Seventh Ave. & Broadway.
www.timessquarebid.org.
Spectacular billboards aren't just an option in Times Square; they're mandated by law. New York's commercial heart is ablaze day and night with stores and vendors vying for visitors' attention. One of the newest dazzlers is **Toys R Us** *(1514 Broadway; 646-366-8822; www.toysrus.com),* where kids can ride a 60ft Ferris wheel and greet Barbie in a life-size town house.

Orchard Street★

Between Delancey & E. Houston Sts.
The commercial spine of Manhattan's Lower East Side, is chock-a-block with boutiques and galleries. Check out the area between Delancey and East Houston and you'll find plenty of one-of-a-kind bargains. It's especially nice on Sundays, when Orchard Street is closed to cars.

Bridgemarket

59th St. & First Ave.

An immense, cathedral-like hall under the roadway to the Queensboro Bridge has been restored to its original grandeur, thanks to the efforts of British designer Terrence Conran, who in the early 1990s signed on to develop a shop and restaurant on the site. Credit for the glorious results goes largely to the father-and-son team Rafael and Rafael Guastavino, who covered the vaulted ceilings with thousands of clay tiles.

- **Conran's** *(407 E. 59th St.; 212-755-7249; www.conran.com)* houseware and design emporium is a favorite among design-conscious bargain hunters.

- **Gustavino's** *(409 E. 59th St.; 212-980-2455; www.gustavinos.com)* 300-seat brasserie serves creative American cuisine; in summer, dine on the pretty outdoor terrace.

Neighborhoods for Shopping

Crystal District – In 2002 the city unveiled its newest shopping destination: a five-block stretch of Madison Avenue *(from 58th to 63rd Sts.)* that's now home to the world's richest concentration of crystal decorative objects and jewelry.

The Sparkling Lineup *(addresses below are on Madison Ave.)*

- **Baccarat** *(no. 625; 212-826-4100; www.baccarat.fr)* traces its lineage back to 1764. Its 4,500sq ft US flagship has two floors of sparkling wares.

- **Daum** *(no. 694; 212-355-2060)* has been around for 120 years and showcases designs specially created by avant-garde artists, including Salvador Dalí.

- **Lalique** *(no. 712; 212-355-6550; www.lalique.com)* offers crystal as well as luxury goods including silk scarves, perfume and porcelain.

- **Steuben** *(no. 667; 212-752-1441; www.steuben.com)* moved to this location in May 2002, selling its trademark animal figurines as well as bowls and vases.

- **Swarovski** *(no. 625; 212-308-1710; www.swarovski.com)*, a family-owned company based in Austria is the world's leading manufacturer of full-cut crystal.

Nolita – *Mulberry, Mott, & Elizabeth Sts. between Kenmare & Houston Sts.*
For shopaholics, the acronym for "North of Little Italy" has become synonymous with fashion daring and originality. In recent years, young designers fleeing the high rents of SoHo have turned Little Italy pizzerias and shoe-repair businesses into trendy boutiques. See for yourself what all the fuss is about.

SoHo – *Bounded by Canal, W. Houston & Crosby Sts., and W. Broadway.*
Try walking down SoHo's narrow sidewalks on a sunny Saturday and you'll see what this 26-block historic district is *really* famous for. High-end boutiques have brought in world-class architects to transform their storefronts into glittering showplaces—check out Rem Koolhaas's space-age dressing rooms inside Prada *(575 Broadway)*. Among the 100 other shops, you'll find Mac Cosmetics, DKNY, and Vivienne Westwood. Outside, vendors display jewelry and knock-off designer items.

Sample Sales

One of the best ways to get designer clothes at rock-bottom prices in New York is to attend a sample sale or a trunk sale. This is when designers unload everything that didn't make it into mass production. Elbows can be sharp, but the savings are fantastic. Check *New York Magazine* or *Time Out New York* for this week's sales.

More Stores

Bloomingdale's – *1000 3rd Ave., between 59th & 60th Sts. 212-705-2098. www.bloomingdales.com.* "Bloomie's," as it's affectionately called, has been an Upper East Side mecca for decades. Here, high fashion applies not only to clothes but to all the merchandise, from designer bonbons to chic shower curtains.

Century 21 – *22 Cortlandt St., between Broadway & Church Sts. 212-227-9092. www.c21stores.com.* You won't find the gracious service here that you'll find at the Fifth Avenue department stores, but you will find savings of 40 to 70 percent on top-shelf brands. Be prepared for a little chaos—New Yorkers love it!

Macy's – *Herald Square (6th Ave. & 34th St.). 212-695-4400. www.macys.com.* The world's largest department store holds 2.1 million square feet of space and more than 500,000 different items. The store's so big (and historic) that it even has a visitor center *(34th St. balcony)* with information about where to find what in the store and the city.

Zabar's – *2245 Broadway at 80th St., Upper West Side. 212-787-2000. www.zabar.com.* No ordinary grocery store, Zabar's is world renowned for its selection of gourmet treats. Though it started as a Jewish deli, it now stretches a city block and sells unusual foods from around the globe, including more than 600 varieties of imported cheeses. Dip inside for ready-to-eat chicken pot pie, Texas barbecue ribs and onion-crusted salmon fillets. Or bring home a chocolate babka for a friend. They'll love you for it.

Outdoor Shopping

Some of the best shopping in the city takes place outdoors, where you can enjoy the fresh (okay, maybe not so fresh) air and feel the pulse of the city streets. In addition to the **Union Square Greenmarket** *(see Parks)*, try the **26th Street Flea Market** in Chelsea *(see Neighborhoods)*, where you'll discover an awesome variety of furniture, vintage clothes and tchotchkes . You can buy both antiques and farm-fresh produce at the **Green Flea Market**, held each Sunday on the Upper West Side *(Columbus Ave. at 77th St.)*. Be sure to bargain—it might not work but it's worth a try.

Must Be Seen: Nightlife

Jump on the subway at three or four in the morning and you'll find the rumor is true: New York really *is* the city that never sleeps. Gotham comes alive each night in its pubs and clubs, many offering music and live entertainment. Here's a selection of some of the most atmospheric venues. Check local listings for what's on tap when you're in town.

Bemelmans Bar – *35 E. 76th St. at Madison Ave. 212-744-1600. www.thecarlyle.com.* The sister venue of Cafe Carlyle *(below)* recently got a makeover that deepened its Rat Pack-era allure. Cocoon-like banquettes make listening to jazz here a decadent experience.

Blue Note Jazz Club – *131 W. 3rd St., between 6th Ave. & MacDougal Sts. 212-475-8592. www.bluenote.net.* Incredible acoustics, an intimate setting and a stellar lineup (often two top artists in one evening) make this one of the city's best jazz clubs. Continental cuisine is served late.

Bottom Line – *25 W. 4th St. 212-228-7880. www.bottomlinecabaret.com.* Rock, folk, and jazz musicians flock to this Village institution, where the small stage belies the big names that show up—sometimes unannounced.

Cafe Carlyle – *35 E. 76th St. at Madison Ave. 212-744-1600. www.thecarlyle.com.* Seeing a show at the Carlyle is one of *the* things to do in New York City. Regular acts include crooner Bobby Short and Woody Allen, who plays clarinet with the Eddy Davis New Orleans Jazz Band.

Gotham Comedy Club – *34 W. 22nd St., between Fifth & Sixth Aves. 212-367-9000. www.gothamcomedyclub.com.* One of New York's leading stand-up clubs, Gotham hosts everyone from unknowns to celebrities—as long as they're funny. You be the judge. Jerry Seinfeld has been known to drop in here to test-drive his new material.

Iridium Jazz Club – *1650 Broadway at 51st St. 212-582-2121. www.iridiumjazzclub.com.* This relative newcomer to New York's jazz scene has won fans with its impressive roster of artists and its 600-bottle wine list.

Jazz Standard – *116 E. 27th St., between Lexington & Park Aves. 212-576-2232. www.jazzstandard.net.* There's no minimum food or drink order here, because the owners are certain you'll want baby back ribs and pan-fried catfish from Blue Smoke restaurant upstairs. Superlative bookings and crystalline sound make this a great choice.

Joe's Pub – *425 Lafayette St. 212-539-8777. www.publictheater.org.* Named in honor of Public Theater founder Joseph Papp, Joe's Pub has become the leading downtown venue for cabaret acts. Two shows a night.

King Kong Room – *240 W. 47th St. 212-921-1940. www.kingkongroom.com.* Thanks to the rollicking success of Jim Caruso's after-curtain "cast parties," this Theater District lounge now hosts two shows every Monday night. Come hear Broadway performers try to impress each other at the mike.

Knitting Factory – *74 Leonard St., between Broadway & Church Sts. 212-228-8490. www.knittingfactory.com.* Legendary home of the musical avant-garde, the club hosts live jazz and rock upstairs, more experimental music below—and 18 beers on tap.

Lenox Lounge – *288 Lenox Ave. (between 124th & 125th Sts.). 212-427-0253. www.lenoxlounge.com.* Film producers looking for an authentic Harlem club of the 1920s find what they need at the Lounge. Patrons include both locals and downtowners.

Luna Lounge – *171 Ludlow St. 212-260-2323. www.eatingit.net.* "Eating it at the Luna Lounge" doesn't refer to dining; it's the name of the Monday-night comedy series that's ridiculously cheap *($7 includes a free drink)* and often entertaining ("eating it" is slang for bombing).

The Steakhouse at Monkey Bar – *In the Hotel Elysée, 60 E. 54th St. (between Park & Madison Aves.). 212-838-2600. www.elyseehotel.com.* Try a sparkling monkey (champagne and Chambord) in this beautifully restored former haunt of author Tennessee Williams and actress Tallulah Bankhead.

Pianos – *158 Ludlow St. 212-505-3733.* Housed in a former piano shop, this wallet-friendly, starkly minimalist new-comer books an impressive lineup of DJs and garage-rock bands.

S.O.B.'s (Sounds of Brazil) – *204 Varick St. at Houston St. 212-243-4940. www.sobs.com.* New York's premier world-music venue has a tropical decor, a cabana-like bar, and a menu with tasty Brazilian and Portuguese specialties. When the music starts pumping, the crowd hits the dance floor.

No Smoking
Since April 2003, almost all bars and clubs in New York have been made smoke-free by law. Exceptions include places that make more than 10 percent of their money through tobacco sales. If you want to light up indoors, try **Circa Tabac** *(32 Watts St.; 212-941-1781)*, where an efficient ventilation system keeps the fumes to a minimum.

Tonic – *107 Norfolk St. 212-358-7501. www.tonicny.com.* What used to be a kosher winery on the Lower East Side has become one of the city's leading purveyors of contemporary music. The old wine casks in the basement have been turned into booths.

Village Vanguard – *178 Seventh Ave. S. 212-255-4037. www.villagevanguard.com.* Photographs of Bill Evans and other jazz greats line the walls, and top-billing jazz musicians take the stage at New York's oldest jazz club, in Greenwich Village. Musicians often drop in after their gigs at other clubs for late-night jam sessions.

Must Be Pampered: Spas

A trip to New York can sometimes feel as hectic as staying at home, but it doesn't have to be that way. Whether you're fighting jet lag or aching after days of pounding pavements, a visit to one of these spas can be just what the doctor ordered.

Acqua Beauty Bar

7 E. 14th St. 212-620-4329. www.acquabeautybar.com.

Think you're already on vacation? Think again. Acqua Beauty Bar offers a range of "journeys" for the face, body and nails. Treatments range from the Temple of the Soul massage to high-tech facials (Compu-Lift, microdermabrasion). There's even a "decolletage panacea" for people who need to "regain balance."

Ajune

1294 Third Ave., between 74th & 75th Sts. 212-628-0044. www.ajune.com.

Aestheticians at this Uptown oasis offer personalized treatments for the muscle-sore and wrinkle-weary. Low-tech solutions include the facial *du jour*, which draws on the curative powers of fresh fruits and essential oils; and the ginger massage, which uses moisture and heat to work out all that tension. For those wanting eternal youth—or at least the appearance of it—there are botox and collagen injections.

Bliss Spa

558 Broadway at Prince St., 2nd floor; 19 E. 57th St., 3rd floor. 212-219-8970. www.blissworld.com.

Since opening its first tiny outpost in SoHo in 1996, Bliss has become one of New York's leading purveyors of decadence and relaxation. The ultimate skin and massage treatment is the Ginger Rub. You'll be slathered in crushed ginger and essential oils, then wrapped in foil and left to steep on a bed of hot water. Afterward, a comprehensive 100-minute massage. Ahhh.

Carapan Urban Spa

5 W. 16th St., between Fifth & Sixth Aves. 212-633-6220. www.carapan.com.

Stressed-out New Yorkers love this cool, Southwestern-style spa, whose name means "a beautiful place of tranquility where one comes to restore one's spirit." The candlelit, incense-scented atmosphere is the perfect backdrop for rejuvenating treatments ranging from aromatherapy facials to the combination Swedish-shiatsu massage. For all-over pore cleansing, reserve time in the sauna.

Graceful Services

1097 Second Ave. at 57th St. 212-593-9904. www.gracefulservices.com.

If it's simple pleasures you're after, head here for a relaxing rubdown. A basic Qi Gong massage (which focuses on vital points on the body to increase circulation) at this simple outfit runs only about $60.

John Allan's Club

46 E. 46th St., 212-922-0361; 95 Trinity Pl., 212-406-3000. www.johnallans.com.

This admirably efficient outfit knows that men need pampering too. The "Full Service" treatment offers a shoe shine, a shampoo, a hair cut, a scalp massage, a hot-towel facial, and a manicure—all for $65. No wonder Wall Street execs and Madison Avenue ad men love this place.

La Prairie Spa

Ritz-Carlton Hotel, 50 Central Park South. 212-308-9100. www.ritz-carlton.com.

Can't slow down enough for a full treatment? Then consider one of La Prairie's Manhattan Minutes spa packages. Jet Lag Therapy includes aromatherapy massage, foot reflexology, and a facial. After-Shopping Paradise blends foot massage with a pedicure. For the one-hour Changing Room special, both you and your clothes get a good steaming, while you're treated to a manicure, a facial and a makeover.

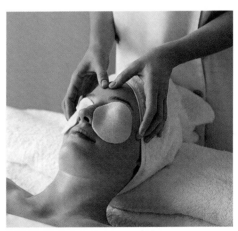

Stone Spa

125 Fourth Ave., between 12th & 13th Sts. 212-254-3045. www.stonespa.com.

Though you can choose anything from a do-it-yourself Maya mud treatment to a full-service antioxidant pomegranate body mask, the specialty here is a hot-stone massage. Therapists glide smooth, heated river stones over your body to melt away tensions and stress and improve circulation. In the summer you can take your treatments in the backyard garden.

Manhattan may be the heart of New York City, but a lot of life goes on in the four "outer" boroughs: the Bronx, Queens, Brooklyn and Staten Island, all of which were incorporated into the city in 1898. Here you'll find not only the vast majority of New Yorkers, but some of New York's best-loved—and least crowded—attractions.

THE BRONX

Home of the New York Yankees (aka "the Bronx Bombers"), the Bronx is New York's only borough located on the mainland. It was named after Jonas Bronck, a Swedish emigré who arrived here in June 1639. Today about half the borough's residents are Hispanic and 25 percent of its acreage is parkland.

Bronx Zoo★★★

Fordham Rd. at Bronx River Pkwy. 718-367-1010. www.wcs.org. Open Apr–Oct Mon–Fri, 10am–5pm, weekends/holidays til 5:30pm; rest of the year open daily 10am–4:30pm. $11. 2 train to Pelham Pkwy.

Bronx Zoo Express

One of the easiest ways to get to the zoo is by bus. The Liberty Lines BXM11 **express bus** *($4; exact change required; no MetroCards; www.libertylines.com)* runs every 20 minutes, picking up along Madison Ave. in Manhattan at 27th, 32nd, 39th, 47th, 54th, 63rd, 70th, 84th and 99th streets. The Bronx Zoo is the next stop after 99th Street.

It's a jungle out there. At least it is at the country's largest urban zoo. Set in a 265-acre woodland park, the Bronx Zoo is so pretty you sometimes forget you're in the company of some of the most magnificent creatures on earth. From elegant ibex to goofy gibbons, the animals here enjoy homes that mirror their natural habitats as much as possible—the Wildlife Conservation Society makes sure of that. The zoo was founded in 1899. Today it showcases more than 4,000 animals and is an important center for researching and breeding endangered species.

Lions and Tigers and Bears—Oh my!

JungleWorld★★ – See Bali mynahs fly among Malayan tapirs, silver leaf monkeys and Indian gharials in this indoor re-creation of an Asian rain forest.

Tiger Mountain★★ – The zoo's spectacular new tiger exhibit puts you just a whisker away from the largest member of the cat family. Meow!

Wild Asia★★ – The Bengali Express Monorail passes through 38 acres populated by free-roaming tigers, gaur cattle, red pandas and rhinoceroses.

Congo Gorilla Forest★ – This 6.5-acre African rain forest counts more than 300 animals, including one of the largest breeding groups of lowland gorillas.

Children's Zoo★ – Here kids can feed domestic farmyard animals and see others in natural environments.

New York Botanical Garden★★

200th St. & Kazimiroff Blvd. 718-817-8700. www.nybg.org. Open Apr–Oct Tue–Sun 10am–6pm, rest of the year Tue–Sun 10am–4pm. Closed Mon, Thanksgiving Day & Dec 25. $3 (additional fees for tram). For access, see sidebar below.

Green thumbs won't want to miss this gorgeous horticultural landmark, located directly north of the Bronx Zoo. Founded in 1891, it is one of the largest and oldest gardens in the country. Numerous walking trails wind through its 250 acres past such favorites as the Rose Garden, the Rock Garden, the Native Plant Garden and the Daylily Collection. The site also features 50 acres of original forest. Peak season is late spring/early summer, though you'll see interesting exhibits and plenty of plants in bloom throughout the year.

Travel Tip

Take the Metro-North Harlem line from Grand Central Station to the Botanical Garden stop, directly outside the garden gate. The trip takes only 20 minutes!

Enid A. Haupt Conservatory★★ – Built in 1901, this glorious Victorian structure showcases global plant communities from rain forests to deserts.

Everett Children's Adventure Garden – Forty hands-on exhibits allow kids and families to explore how plants live and function.

Wave Hill★

675 W. 252nd St. 718-549-3200. www.wavehill.org. Open mid-Apr–mid-Oct Tue–Sun 9am–5:30pm, rest of the year Tue–Sun 9am–4:30pm. Closed Mon & major holidays. $4 (free Tue & mid-Nov–mid-Mar). 1 or 9 train to 231st St., then take Bronx #7 or #10 bus to 252nd St.

From its spectacular perch above the Hudson River, Wave Hill—a gardener's paradise—seems worlds away from the city. This enchanting 28-acre estate was built as a country home in the 1840s and has had some illustrious occupants, including Theodore Roosevelt's family and Mark Twain. Today 18 acres of its grounds have been expertly landscaped into seven separate gardens, containing more than 3,200 species. Must-sees here include the herb garden, the alpine garden, the dry garden, the wild garden, the pergola and the conservatory.

Yankee Stadium★

161st St. & River Ave. See Musts for Fun (stadium tour) and Practical Information (tickets & schedule).

BROOKLYN

New York's most populous borough occupies the western tip of Long Island. Founded by the Dutch in 1636, the area was named Breuckelen ("broken land") after a small town near Utrecht. The population exploded after the Brooklyn Bridge opened in 1883. Today Brooklyn is a mix of separate neighborhoods, from hipster Williamsburg to staid Brooklyn Heights to honky-tonk Coney Island to verdant Park Slope—the most recent haven for the diaper-and-stroller crowd.

Brooklyn Bridge★★★ — *Adjacent to South Street Seaport. See Landmarks.*

Brooklyn Botanic Garden★★

900 Washington Ave. 718-623-7200. www.bbg.org. Open Apr–Sept Tue–Fri 8am–6pm, weekends 10am–6pm, rest of the year Tue–Fri 8am–4:30pm, weekends 10am–4:30pm. Closed Mon & major holidays. $3. 2 or 3 train to Eastern Pkwy.; Q train to Prospect Park.

Bordering the east edge of Prospect Park and serving as a de facto backyard for the Brooklyn Museum of Art, this refreshing oasis covers 52 acres and includes one of the finest assemblages of roses in the country. Its outdoor gardens are separated into nine distinct styles, including a Shakespeare garden and a Japanese garden. The Steinhardt Conservatory houses the country's largest bonsai collection.

Brooklyn Heights★★

If you decide to walk over the Brooklyn Bridge, consider taking a stroll around this lovely neighborhood at the other end. It's a wealthy enclave of narrow, tree-lined streets bordered with historic brownstones. Willow and Pierrepont

streets are particularly picturesque. Montague Street is the commercial strip, with cafes and high-end boutiques. And don't miss the **esplanade**, which runs along the East River from Montague to Orange Street and affords magnificent views of the Financial District across the river.

Walking Tours

If you want an insider's view of Brooklyn, the **Brooklyn Historical Society** *(128 Pierrepont St.; 718-222-4111; www.brooklynhistory.org)* organizes walking tours of the area. They also maintain the borough's only history museum.

Brooklyn Museum of Art★★

*200 Eastern Pkwy.
718-638-5000.
www.brooklynmuseum.org.
Open year-round Wed–Fri
10am–5pm, weekends
11am–6pm. Closed Mon,
Tue, Jan 1, Thanksgiving Day
& Dec 25. $6. 2 or 3 train to
Eastern Pkwy.*

Best known for its Egyptian collection and its superb cache of American paintings, the Brooklyn Museum is the second-largest art museum in the US. It illustrates art history from ancient times to the present with selections from its 1.5-million-piece collection. The monumental Beaux-Arts structure, designed by McKim, Mead and White, was opened in 1897 but has been undergoing modifications throughout its existence. The latest round has brought some huge improvements. In 2003 viewing space for the Egyptian collection doubled, the Beaux-Arts Court displaying European painting was totally refurbished, and a public study center for the museum's splendid collection of American art was opened. Now underway is a complete restoration of the facade and the addition of an entrance pavilion, to be completed in 2004.

First Floor – African art, pre-Columbian art of the Americas, and Oceanic art.

Second Floor – Asian and Islamic art, including Chinese jades and Persian carpets.

Third Floor – The stunning **Egyptian art collection**★★ is arranged thematically and chronologically; European paintings range from the Italian Renaissance to the early 20C, with a good selection of Impressionists.

Fourth Floor – American period rooms; costumes and textiles.

Fifth Floor – American paintings by Cole, Copley, Eakins, Homer, Sargent, Cassatt and O'Keeffe sit shoulder-to-shoulder with sculpture and decorative arts. Here you'll also find 58 sculptures by Rodin.

Prospect Park★

Entrance at Grand Army Plaza, intersection of Flatbush Ave. & Prospect Park W. 718-965-8967. www.prospectpark.org.

After a visit to the museum, check out Brooklyn's most cherished park, a 526-acre wonderland of meadows and woods, lakes and streams designed in 1896 by Olmsted and Vaux, creators of Central Park. A road traces its periphery, and paths cut through its interior, which has plenty of ball parks and recreation facilities, as well as a carousel, a band shell and a small zoo. For lunch, exit the west side of the park and go two blocks to **Seventh Avenue**, a family-friendly strip of restaurants, cafes and boutiques.

New York Aquarium★★

W. 8th St. & Surf Ave., Coney Island. 718-265-3474. www.nyaquarium.com. Open Apr–May & Sept–Oct, Mon–Fri 10am–5pm (weekends & holidays until 5:30pm); May–Sept 10am–6pm (weekends until 7pm). $11. W train to Stillwell Ave.

The weather outside might be frightful, but for the aquatic creatures at this indoor-outdoor facility, the water is always delightful. The first New York Aquarium—reputedly the first aquarium in the US—opened in 1896 in what is now Castle Clinton National Monument *(see Historic Sites)*. The present facility, administered by the Wildlife Conservation Society, has been a Coney Island institution since 1957. In large outdoor pools, whales, seals, sea lions, dolphins and Pacific walrus go through their paces *(check at entrance for feeding schedule)*. Indoor aquariums display more than 8,000 specimens and 300 species from around the world.

Alien Stingers – Unveiled in fall 2002, the exhibit showcases sea jellies, corals and anemones.

Conservation Hall – Cownose rays glide through a floor-to-ceiling tank.

Sea Cliffs – The 300ft-long North Pacific coastline habitat contains penguins, mullets, sea horses, walruses, octopuses and other creatures that can be viewed above and below the water.

Verrazano-Narrows Bridge★★

Toll: $8 per car, paid only on westbound crossing. R train to 95th St. & 4th Ave.

The longest suspension bridge in the US, this mammoth structure links Brooklyn to Staten Island above the Narrows (the entrance to New York Harbor) and marks the starting point of the annual New York Marathon. The bridge bears the name of Italian explorer Giovanni da Verrazano, who discovered the site of New York in 1524. The engineer was O.H. Amman, who also designed the George Washington Bridge. Work on the bridge began in 1959. Upon its completion in 1964, urban planner Robert Moses called it a "triumph of simplicity and restraint."

Bridging The Facts

The bridge boasts a total length of 13,700ft. The main span between the tower extends 4,260ft. The main cables are 3ft in diameter (nearly 2 ½ times the girth of the Brooklyn Bridge's cables). There are two levels for car traffic but no sidewalk for pedestrians. If you want to hoof it, you have to run the marathon!

Brooklyn Academy of Music★ – *30 Lafayette Ave. See Performing Arts.*

QUEENS

With an area of 120sq mi and a population topping two million, New York's biggest borough draws thousands of immigrants each year to its relatively affordable housing and its tight-knit ethnic communities—but for years it wasn't much of a draw for tourists. That is slowly changing as film studios and art museums make use of abandoned factories in the Long Island City and Astoria neighborhoods. Inland, sports thrive at Shea Stadium (home of the New York Mets), the USTA National Tennis Center (where the US Open is played each September) and Aqueduct Racetrack (thoroughbred horse racing). Of course, many visitors come here whether they want to or not: LaGuardia and Kennedy airports are both in Queens.

Museum of Modern Art/MoMA QNS★★★

45-20 33rd St. at Queens Blvd. See Museums.

Isamu Noguchi Garden Museum★★

32-37 Vernon Blvd., Long Island City. 718-204-7088. www.noguchi.org. The museum is closed for renovation until April 2004. N train to Broadway or take the Artlink bus (see p 102).

Sculptor Isamu Noguchi designed and used this factory space as a studio before making it a permanent museum of his works in 1985. Noguchi began his artistic career in 1935 as a set designer for modern-dance guru Martha Graham. Later he sculpted a range of works, from the stainless-steel *News* for the entrance of the Associated Press building at 50 Rockefeller Center to Atlanta's *Playscapes*. Set to reopen in April 2004 after extensive renovations, this museum displays 250 of Noguchi's works in stone, wood, clay and metal, as well as working models for many of his large-scale public projects.

P.S. 1 Contemporary Art Center

22-25 Jackson Ave. at 46th Ave. 718-784-2084. www.ps1.org. Open year-round Wed–Sun noon–6pm. $5 donation. 7 local train to Courthouse Square; E or V train to 23rd St./Ely Ave.

An affiliate of MoMA since 1999, P.S. 1 has been operating out of this 1893 school building (the "P.S." stands for "public school") since 1976. The five-story center nurtures new talent and has a cutting-edge approach to shows. You'll usually find at least one site-specific installation here as well as something from MoMA, which uses the mammoth space to display large-scale works. The rest is up in the air—that's the fun of it.

American Museum of the Moving Image★

35th Ave. at 36th St. in Astoria. 718-784-0077. www.movingimage.us. Open year-round Tue–Fri noon–5pm, weekends 11am–6pm. Closed Mon, Tue & major holidays. $8.50. R, V or G train to Steinway St.

Both cinephiles and tech-happy kids will be happy here. This eye-popping place uses its trove of film-related paraphernalia to describe the art, craft and business of making moving images. What is a moving image? Well, in AMMI's view, it's anything from a flip book to Pac-Man, though much of the space between is (gratefully) taken up by film. The museum was founded in 1988 in a portion of the former Kaufman Astoria Studios, which were built by Paramount Pictures in the 1920s and used by Paul Robeson, the Marx brothers and Rudolph Valentino. The studios were abandoned in 1971 but revived in the 1990s and now bustle with film and television shoots. Though that part of the complex is off limits, the museum describes a lot of the activity going on there. Repertory films are shown every weekend.

Behind the Screen – The AMMI's core exhibition lets you record voice-over dialogue and try your hand at other aspects of getting a moving image made.

Digital Media – Here you can sample some of the latest computer graphics technology.

Museum for African Art★

36-01 43rd Ave., 3rd floor, Long Island City. 718-784-7700. www.africanart.org. Open year-round Mon, Thu & Fri 10am–5pm, weekends 11am–6pm. Closed Tue, Wed & major holidays. $5. 7 local train to 33rd St.

Located only three blocks from MoMA QNS, this 20-year-old museum is the only independent museum in the country dedicated to African art and culture. It specializes in curating exhibitions of African art, drawing pieces from various collections (the museum has just started its own collection). Many shows blend contemporary with traditional works, including painting, sculpture, textiles and masks, to explore a question or theme. The Main Gallery has long-term exhibitions, while the Focus Gallery changes about six times a year.

Queens Artlink

212-708-9750. www.queensartlink.org. A second Artlink shuttle connects MoMA QNS (see Museums/Museum of Modern Art) to P.S. 1, the American Museum of the Moving Image, the Isamu Noguchi Museum and the Museum for African Art.

STATEN ISLAND

Sometimes referred to as "the forgotten borough," Staten Island is primarily a bedroom community, sharing more in common with New Jersey than with New York. Still, the Staten Island Ferry is a thrilling—and free—ride, and while you're over there, you might as well take a look around.

Alice Austen House Museum★

2 Hylan Blvd. 718-816-4506. www.aliceausten.org. Open Mar–Dec Thu–Sun noon–5pm. Closed Jan, Feb & major holidays. $2. From the ferry terminal, take S51 bus to Hylan Blvd.

Pioneer photographer Alice Austen (1866–1952) captured turn-of-the-century life in New York City, snapping elite society gatherings and immigrant scenes alike. Restored according to her own pictures, this Victorian cottage displays changing exhibits, including prints from her glass-plate negatives.

Historic Richmond Town★

441 Clarke Ave. 718-351-1611. www.historicrichmondtown.org. Open Jul–Aug Wed–Fri 10am–5pm, weekends 1pm–5pm. Rest of the year Wed–Sun 1pm–5pm. Closed Mon, Tue & major holidays. $4. From the ferry terminal, take S74 bus.

Summertime is "living-history season" at this 25-acre village, with costumed interpreters demonstrating crafts (tinsmithing, printmaking) and telling stories about life in the former county seat. Exhibits in the **Staten Island Historical Society Museum** relate the history of the island.

Jacques Marchais Museum of Tibetan Art★

338 Lighthouse Ave. 718-987-3500. www.tibetanmuseum.com. Open year-round Wed–Sun 1pm–5pm. Closed Mon, Tue, Thanksgiving Day & Dec 25–Jan 1. $5. From the ferry terminal, take S74 bus.

Here you'll find a rare collection of art and artifacts from Tibet, Nepal, China, Mongolia and India in an enchanting setting. Topping Lighthouse Hill amid terraced gardens and lily ponds, the museum buildings resemble a small Buddhist mountain temple.

Staten Island Ferry★

Departs from Whitehall Terminal, at the southern tip of Battery Park in Manhattan, for the St. George Terminal on Staten Island, daily year-round, about every 30min. 718-812-2628. siferry.com. $3/car (on foot, free). 1 or 9 train to South Ferry; N or R train to Whitehall St.

Who said there were no free rides in life? The Staten Island Ferry, which shuttles commuters back and forth between Manhattan and "the forgotten borough," is free—and it offers some of the best views of Manhattan and the Statue of Liberty that you're likely to find at any price. On the windy voyage,  which covers 5mi and takes 25 minutes each way, the boat skirts the Statue of Liberty. On the return trip, you can zoom in on the lower New York skyline.

You'll be surprised how quickly the city melts away as you head north along the Hudson River or east out to Long Island. Drive north along US-9 and you'll discover a rich landscape of highlands and history. If you're craving the feel of sand between your toes, jump on the Long Island Parkway to reach some of the finest beaches and best-protected harbors on the Atlantic Coast.

HUDSON RIVER VALLEY★★★

Tarrytown, the southern limit of the valley, is 30mi north of New York City. Take I-87 North as it becomes the New York Thruway. For the east side of the river, take Saw Mill Pkwy. North. to Rte. 9 or 9W. Tourist information: Hudson Valley Tourism (800-232-4782; www.travelhudsonvalley.org) or Historic Hudson Valley (914-631-8200; www.hudsonvalley.org). Historic homes can only be visited by guided tour.

A remarkable concentration of historic homes in the Hudson River Valley reflects the early 17C Dutch settlement pattern that carved feudal estates, called "patroonships," out of the land flanking the river. When the English took over in 1664, they turned these estates into lordly manors. In the 1800s the region's wild beauty inspired artists of the Hudson River school—including Frederic Edwin Church, Thomas Cole, and Albert Bierstadt—to paint massive landscapes. Today you'll find rocky crags and wooded peaks surrounding historic mansions, and small towns (Cold Spring, Rhinebeck) nestling near the riverbanks, chock-a-block with antiques stores.

Boscobel Restoration★★

1601 Rte. 4D, Garrison. 914-265-3638. www.boscobel.org. Open Apr–Oct Mon, Wed–Sun 9:30am–5pm. Nov–Dec Mon, Wed–Sun 9:30am–4pm. Closed Jan–Mar, Tue, Thanksgiving Day & Dec 25. $8.

Fans of the Federal style love this elegant manor, which was built in the early 1800s but moved in pieces to this site overlooking the Hudson in the 1950s. The restored interior features graceful arches, fireplaces embellished with classical motifs, delicately carved woodwork and Duncan Phyfe furnishings.

Castle at Tarrytown
400 Benedict Ave., Tarrytown. 914-631-1980 or 800-616-4487. www.castleattarrytown.com. 31 rooms. Over $300. Resembling a medieval castle with its towers and arched windows, this 1910 mansion-turned-inn tops a hill overlooking the Hudson, 25mi north of New York City. Inside, period tapestries soften the stone walls, and hand-carved four-poster beds and custom-made chandeliers decorate the guest rooms. Save time for a meal at **Equus**, where you'll dine on memorable French cuisine.

Home of FDR National Historic Site★★

US-9, Hyde Park. 845-229-9115. www.nps.gov/hofr. Open year-round daily 9am–4:30pm. Closed Jan 1, Thanksgiving Day, and Dec 25. $10.

You'll feel as if you know the Roosevelt family personally after a visit to this estate, which is bursting with historic memorabilia. Franklin Delano Roosevelt's father bought the site in 1867, and FDR was born here in 1882. In the rose garden, a simple monument of white Vermont marble marks the final resting place of FDR and his wife, Eleanor.

Take The Boat

Did you know that Kykuit and West Point are both accessible by boat? NY Waterway offers full-day Hudson cruises from Manhattan, with stops at these and other historic sites. *For more information: 800-533-3779 or nywaterway.com.*

Kykuit★★

US-9, Sleepy Hollow. 914-631-3992. www.hudsonvalley.org. Open late Apr–early Nov Wed–Mon 10am–4pm. Closed Jan–Mar, Tue, Thanksgiving Day & Dec 25. $20.

Dutch for "lookout," Kykuit (pronounced "KYE-cut") is the most picturesque of the Hudson Valley estates. It's also one of the newest. The house was built between 1906 and 1913 by John D. Rockefeller Jr. for his father, the patriarch of Standard Oil; in all, Kykuit has housed four generations of Rockefellers. Inside you'll find no less than antique Chinese porcelain and tapestries by Pablo Picasso. The lovely terraced **grounds**★ contain sculptures by such artists as Picasso, Louise Nevelson and Isamu Noguchi.

West Point★★

West Bank. Rte. 218 S., West Point. 845-938-2638. www.usma.edu. Grounds may be visited by guided tour only Apr–Oct Mon–Sat & holidays 10am–3:30pm, Sun 11am–3:30pm. Rest of the year daily 11:15am & 1:15pm. Tour information: 845-446-4724 or www.westpointtours.com. $7.

The prestigious US Military Academy was established here in 1802, on the site of Fortress West Point, a 1778 series of fortifications overlooking the Hudson at one of its most narrow points. In 1780 Benedict Arnold, the fort's commander, schemed to hand West Point over to the British (the plan was thwarted). In the academy's first year, 10 students graduated; today there are more than 4,200 cadets here. Try to plan your visit to coincide with one of the academy's spectacular **parades**, known for their precision of movement *(Sept–Nov & late Apr–May)*. And be sure to visit the **museum**★★, where you'll find out everything you ever wanted to know about the history of the military.

LONG ISLAND★★

Oyster Bay is about 34mi east of New York City. Take the Midtown Tunnel to the Long Island Expwy. (I-495) East. For the north shore, take Rte. 106 North to Rte. 25A. Tourist information: Long Island Convention and Visitors Bureau; 631-951-3440; www.licvb.com.

From end to end, Long Island is a study in extremes. On the western tip you have ultra-urban Brooklyn and Queens; on the eastern tip, the dramatic bluffs of Montauk. In between are vast tracts of suburban development. But that's not all. Long Island boasts many sandy beaches and seafaring towns. Although the North Shore is rockier and more dramatic than the South Shore (which is protected by several long, sandy barrier islands), both are worth exploring.

The Hamptons★★

South Shore. To reach the Hamptons, take I-495 East to Rte. 454 to Rte. 27. Southampton is about 95mi east of New York City. www.thehamptons.com.

Home to the glitterati, Long Island's most renowned vacation spot forms a loose-knit chain of towns running 35mi along the South Shore, from Westhampton Beach to Amagansett. Try tony **Southampton**★ for superb estates and pricey shops, and the port of **Sag Harbor**★ *(northeast of Southampton via Rtes. 27 & 79; 631-725-0011; www.sagharborchamber.com)* for charm. A 15mi-long **public beach** runs from Moriches Inlet to Shinnecock Inlet.

Long Island Museum of American Art, History, and Carriages★★

1200 Rte. 25A, Stony Brook. 631-751-0066. www.longislandmuseum.org. Open year-round Wed–Sat 10am–5pm, Sun noon–5pm. Closed Mon, Tue & major holidays. $5.

This kid-friendly complex has three museums, a blacksmith shop, a schoolhouse and a barn. Plan on spending most of your time in the carriage museum, ogling the 250 horse-drawn carriages that range from Gypsy wagons to children's vehicles (pulled by goats or dogs).

Old Bethpage Village Restoration★★

1303 Round Swamp Rd. Old Bethpage. 516-572-8400. www.oldbethpage.org. Open Jun–Oct Wed–Sun 10am–5pm. Nov–Dec & Mar–May Wed–Sun 10am–4pm. Closed Jan, Feb, Mon & Tue. $7.

Take a stroll through this pre-Civil War village and watch the weaver make cloth, the farmwife prepare a meal, and farmers work their fields. More than 55 historic buildings have been moved to the site, creating a museum that's especially fun for families.

Lobster Roll

1980 Montauk Hwy., Amagansett. 631-267-3740. Closed Nov–mid-Apr. Sand dunes may surround this highway shanty, but don't let the beachy atmosphere fool you. The famous lobster rolls draw the likes of Barbra Streisand, Kathleen Turner and Alec Baldwin.

Planting Fields★★

Planting Fields Rd., Oyster Bay. 516-922-9200. www.plantingfields.com.
Grounds open year-round daily 9am–5pm. Closed Dec 25. $5/car.

Flower power rules at financier William Robertson Coe's former estate, 160 acres of which have been turned into an arboretum. More than 600 rhododendron and azalea species flower here in May and June, and the camellia collection is the oldest and largest of its kind under glass *(in bloom Feb–Mar)*.

Cold Spring Harbor Whaling Museum★

Main St., Cold Spring Harbor. 631-367-3418. www.cshwhalingmuseum.org.
Open late May–Labor Day daily 11am–5pm. Closed Labor Day–Memorial Day. $3.

Fun for kids, this museum brings back the town's 1850s heyday as a whaling port. Exhibits include a fully equipped 19C whaleboat, harpoons, navigational instruments, an orca skull and scrimshaw (whalebone carvings), the whaler's folk art.

Sagamore Hill National Historic Site★

Cove Neck Rd., Oyster Bay. 516-922-4447. www.nps.gov/sahi. Open late May–Labor Day daily 9am–5pm. Rest of the year Wed–Sun 9am–5pm. Closed Mon & major holidays. $5.

This 1885 Queen Anne mansion is maintained as it was during Theodore Roosevelt's presidency (1901–1909), housing more than 90 percent of the family's original furnishings—note the rhinoceros-foot inkstand in Teddy's study, which was a hunting trophy.

Vanderbilt Museum★

Little Neck Rd., Centerport. 631-854-5555. www.vanderbiltmuseum.org. Open year-round daily noon–4pm. Closed Jan 1, Thanksgiving Day & Dec 25. $8.

William K. Vanderbilt II—"Willie K"—was a lifelong traveler, expert yachtsman and racecar driver. The 24-room, Spanish Revival-style mansion is a good setting for the natural history collections on view in the Habitat Wing. There's also a revolving turntable for Vanderbilt's custom-built 1928 Lincoln touring car, a marine museum with ship models, and a planetarium.

Beaches Of Long Island

Had enough of history? Then hit the beach. On the North Shore, **Sunken Meadow State Park**★ *(631-269-4333; www.nysparks.com)* has a large, fine-sand beach as well as recreational activities like hiking and golf. On the South Shore you can choose from **Jones Beach State Park**★★ *(516-785-1600; www.nysparks.com)*, a barrier island boasting 6.5mi of beaches along ocean and bay; automobile-free **Fire Island**★, which encompasses 1,400 acres of **Fire Island National Seashore**★ *(631-289-4810; www.nps.gov/fiis)* and an idyllic beachfront state park; or the **Hamptons**★★.

The venues listed below were selected for their ambience, location and/or value for money. Rates indicate the average cost of an appetizer, an entrée and a dessert for one person (not including tax, gratuity or beverages). Most restaurants are open daily and accept major credit cards. Call for information regarding reservations, dress code and opening hours. Restaurants listed are located in New York City unless otherwise noted. For a complete listing of restaurants mentioned in this guide, see Index.

$$$$ over $50	$$ $15–$30
$$$ $30–$50	$ under $15

Luxury

Fiamma Osteria $$$$ Italian

206 Spring St. (between Sixth Ave. & Sullivan St.), SoHo. 212-653-0100. www.brguestrestaurants.com.

Glass elevators whisk patrons—who have included Harrison Ford, Bette Midler and Billy Joel—to one of the three levels of this tastefully decorated osteria. Dishes, prepared with the freshest of ingredients, change seasonally, and the wine list includes more than 475 labels. Homemade pastas are in a class by themselves, and dishes like *branzino dell'Atlantico* (pan-seared wild striped bass) show off chef Michael White's talents. Desserts are irresistably decadent.

Firebird $$$$ Russian

365 W. 46th St. (between Eighth & Ninth Aves.), Midtown. Closed Mon. 212-586-0244. www.cityguidemagazine.com/newyorkcity/firebirdrestaurant.htm.

Tsar Nicholas would no doubt feel as comfortable in these three elegantly restored town houses as he did in the Winter Palace, and would probably enjoy the cuisine as much, too—with dishes like Ukrainian borscht, poached sturgeon and chicken Kiev, not to mention seven kinds of caviar. It's a fun place to watch the pre-theater crowd before walking over to a Broadway show. Or stay to catch the complimentary jazz at the adjacent Firebird Lounge.

Gotham Bar and Grill $$$$ New American

*12 E. 12th St. (between Fifth Ave. & University Pl.), Greenwich Village.
212-620-4020. www.gothambarandgrill.com.*

Gotham is consistently rated one of New York's finest restaurants, and for
good reason. Executive chef Alfred Portale fits New York to a tee. The pioneer
of vertical cuisine, he creates innovative, towering "skyscraper" presentations
that are a treat for the eye as well as the palate. Seafood salad is a high-rise
concoction of lobster, scallops, octopus, squid and avocado, crowned with a
ruffle of purple lettuce. Even the rich chocolate desserts stand at attention.
The best bargain in town is Gotham's $20 prix-fixe lunch.

Keens Steakhouse $$$$ Steaks

*72 W. 36th St. (between Fifth & Sixth Aves.), Garment District. Dinner only Sat & Sun.
212-947-3636. www.keenssteakhouse.com.*

A carnivore's delight, Keens serves up big slabs of prime rib, steaks and lamb in
a historic setting. The restaurant opened in 1885, when Herald Square—which
is around the corner—was still the city's Theater District. Keens started out as
a men's dining, drinking and pipe-smoking club for the city's movers and
shakers at the turn of the century, and hanging from the ceiling is the world's
biggest collection of churchwarden clay pipes.

Le Bernardin $$$$ French

*155 W. 51st St. (between Avenue of the Americas & Seventh Ave.), Midtown.
Closed Sun & holidays. 212-554-1515. www.le-bernardin.com.*

Expect to spend serious money at this spacious, elegant restaurant, widely
acclaimed as one of the city's best—it will be worth it. With white tablecloths
and white-glove service, Le Bernardin serves a prix-fixe menu that comes
almost entirely from the sea. Prepare yourself for delicately orchestrated
servings of roast baby lobster tail on asparagus and cèpe risotto, saffron ravioli
of herbed crab meat or a pot-au-feu of black bass accompanied by a julienne
of fresh ginger. *Jackets required.*

Next Door Nobu $$$$ Japanese

105 Hudson St. at Franklin St., TriBeCa. Dinner only. 212-334-4445.
www.myriadrestaurantgroup.com.

Although it's nearly impossible to get a table at the highly acclaimed Nobu, you can sample essentially the same food at a slightly lower cost at Next Door Nobu located right next to the parent restaurant. The emphasis here is on texture—its well-crafted sushi bar of black river rocks, tables of scorched pine and Indonesian market-basket light fixtures harmonize with the sensual pleasures of clawless lobsters, sea urchins, seafood udon (noodles) and mochi ice-cream balls. Next Door Nobu doesn't take reservations—go early to avoid a long wait.

Park Avenue Cafe $$$$ American

100 E. 63rd St., Upper East Side. 212-644-1900. www.parkavenuecafe.com.

Whimsical touches of Americana—a shelf of antique cookie jars, a mural of the US flag, sheaves of wheat—fill this contemporary, Upper East Side restaurant. Chef David Burke's acclaimed menu lists signatures like house-cured pastrami salmon and rack of lamb with potato, leek and goat cheese cannelloni. Don't skip the molded chocolate Park Bench, complete with lamppost.

San Domenico NY $$$ Italian

240 Central Park South (between Seventh Ave. & Broadway), Midtown.
212-265-5959. www.restaurant.com/sandomenicony.

One of your best souvenirs from a visit to New York will be memories of dining at San Domenico. The signature dish, *uovo in raviolo al burro nocciola tartufato* (raviolo of soft egg yolk in truffle butter), delicately satisfies. The fillet of sea-bass poached in a fish and tomato broth reflects the importance placed on the exceptional quality of ingredients, and the remarkable wine list is sure to please the most demanding oenophile. Carrara marble, Poltrona Frau banquettes and Cassina chairs make for a discreetly elegant décor.

Moderate

The Boathouse at Central Park $$$ New American

72nd St. & Park Dr. N., Central Park. 212-517-2233.

One of the city's best-kept secrets is hidden inside Central Park. The lakeside eatery switches from its outdoor veranda in summer to a ski lodge-style interior room during colder months. Dishes reflect the city's melting-pot culture: Atlantic salmon is pan-seared and jumbo lump crab cakes are served with cornichon-and-caper remoulade.

Bridge Café $$$ American

279 Water St. at Dover St., Financial District. 212-227-3344. www.bridgecafenyc.com.

The Bridge Café serves up elegant dishes reflecting the chef's preference for seasonal fare using regional ingredients—pan-roasted lobster with heirloom apple and celery-root salad and spicy lobster broth; saffron-poached halibut with puréed cauliflower and Osetra caviar. It also serves up lots of history—located next to the Brooklyn Bridge and a few blocks from South Street Seaport, this little red wooden building dates back to 1794.

Carmine's $$$ Italian

200 W. 44th St. (between Seventh & Eighth Aves.), Midtown, 212-221-3800;
2450 Broadway (between 90th & 91st Sts.), Upper West Side, 212-362-2200.
www.carminesnyc.com.

If you're traveling in a group this is a good place to come for a hearty dinner of southern Italian favorites like veal saltimbocca, chicken *scarpariello* and shrimp scampi. Hefty portions are dished up family-style, so sharing is de rigueur at Carmine's. The midtown location, in the heart of the theater district, will only take reservations for groups of six or more after 6pm (a similar policy is often imposed at the uptown restaurant). But there's plenty of space at the bar if you have to wait.

Josephina $$$ New American

1900 Broadway at 63rd St., Upper West Side. 212-799-1000. www.josephinanyc.com.

This pleasant restaurant across the street from Lincoln Center is often crowded before performances *(6pm–8pm)*. The focus here is on healthy, natural cuisine with interesting non-dairy, fish and vegetarian options as well as meat dishes. The roasted butternut squash soup is a favorite appetizer, while entrées include items like goat cheese ravioli, pan-roasted farm chicken, sesame-coated yellowfin tuna and standards such as rack of lamb and filet mignon. During summer, try a sidewalk table for Broadway people-watching.

Marseille $$$ Mediterranean

630 Ninth Ave. at 44th St., Hell's Kitchen/Clinton.
212-333-2233. www.marseillenyc.com.

This bustling bistro within walking distance of Times Square is a terrific spot for pre- and post-theater dining. Serving French cuisine with Moroccan, Turkish and Tunisian overtones, Marseille's Art Deco setting with its pastel arches, handmade floor tiles and old zinc bar makes you think you're on the set of *Casablanca*. Seared Moroccan tuna with a spicy crust of peppercorns, sesame seeds, cumin and pistachios typifies the chef's artistry. Broadway headliners often drop by between and after performances.

Mesa Grill
$$$ Southwestern

102 Fifth Ave. (between 15th & 16th Sts.), Union Square/Gramercy Park.
212-807-7400. www.mesagrill.com.

Southwestern cuisine doesn't mean just tacos and burritos, as you'll find in this often-crowded bi-level restaurant. It does mean a hint of spice and Mexican influence, as in the yellow-corn-crusted chile relleno, the New Mexican spice-rubbed pork tenderloin or the crispy whole striped bass, and in side dishes like cilantro-pesto mashed potatoes or sweet potato tamale. Celebrate North America with the all-American wine list and fine selection of Mexican tequilas.

Rock Center Café
$$$ American

20 W. 50th St. at Rockefeller Plaza, Midtown. 212-332-7620.
www.restaurantassociates.com.

Tucked into the recently renovated lower level of Rockefeller Center, the Rock Center Café offers comfortable seating for weary shoppers with its spacious banquettes and upholstered chairs. During winter it also provides a unique view outside its huge windows: the skaters on the Rockefeller Center rink. The menu lists a selection of pastas as well as American standards like salmon, prime rib, chicken and steaks.

Budget

Angelica Kitchen
$$ Vegan

300 E. 12th St. (between First & Second Aves.), East Village. 212-228-2909.

Health-conscious New Yorkers love the creative vegan fare (no meat or dairy) at this popular East Village eatery. Most of the dishes are simply prepared, letting the flavors of the vegetables (usually local and organic) speak for themselves. Many diners cobble together dinner from the wide assortment of salads, grilled vegetables, tofu and breads (the rice-dense cornbread is a meal in itself), though the most flavorful dishes are often the daily specials, which range from savory stews to tamales. If you're eating solo, take a seat at the community table, where you can read or chat with Angelica's regulars.

Bistro Margot
$$ French

26 Prince St. (between Elizabeth & Mott Sts.), SoHo. 212-274-1027.

Simple yet elegant, Bistro Margot is a real find in a neighborhood teeming with attitude. Past the ornate bar the narrow space opens up into a dining room, whose unfinished plank floors and white-washed brick walls covered with French signs make it feel like the genuine article. The tiny courtyard (candlelit at night) is especially pleasant in the summertime. Expect generous portions of the classics, including a delectable poached salmon and white-bean salad and buttery-smooth boudin blanc (veal sausages) with potatoes and onions. Wine by the carafe is a bargain.

Carnegie Delicatessen
$$ Jewish Kosher

854 Seventh Ave., Midtown. 212-757-2245. www.carnegiedeli.com.

It's hard to tell what this kosher deli is more famous for—salty service or mile-high pastrami sandwiches. At this New York institution, it's best to endure the former for the latter. Split a sandwich if you want to save room for the wonderful cheesecake. Be prepared to share your table here—it's all part of the fun. Film buffs will be interested to know that much of Woody Allen's 1983 flick *Broadway Danny Rose* was shot on the premises.

El Cid Tapas
$$ Spanish

322 W. 15th St., Chelsea. 212-929-9332.

Family-owned and run, this unprepossessing spot is the best place in the city to get tapas (small portions of Spanish dishes) and fresh sangria. The dozen tables are jammed together and the bar is crowded, so make reservations to sample unforgettable dishes like white asparagus in vinaigrette, and shrimp grilled in garlic. A complimentary glass of sherry is served after dinner.

Merge
$$ New American

142 W. 10th St. (between Greenwich St. & Waverly Pl.), Greenwich Village. Dinner only. 212-691-7757. www.merge-nyc.com.

Cheerful bouquets and terrific food brighten up this intimate, brick-walled favorite in Greenwich Village. Locals come for seasonal entrées such as lavender-honey-glazed pork loin with marinated beets, or hanger steak with horseradish mashed potatoes. Service is comparable to the city's top restaurants.

Noho Star
$$ International

330 Lafayette St. at Bleecker St., East Village. 212-925-0070. www.nohostar.com.

Situated where the East Village, West Village, Little Italy and SoHo come together, this pleasant, inexpensive restaurant is a good place to stop during an excursion through the area. ("NoHo" stands for north of Houston Street.) Open for breakfast, lunch, dinner and weekend brunch, Noho Star's menu is hard to describe, ranging from sandwiches and burgers to standard American entrées to Asian-influenced dishes to classic Chinese (available at dinner only)—a little bit of something for everyone, as befits its polyglot neighborhood.

Must Eat: Restaurants

Pearl Oyster Bar $$ Seafood

18 Cornelia St. (between W. 4th & Bleecker Sts.), Greenwich Village. Closed Sun. 212-691-8211.

You can't get fresher fish for the price in Manhattan. Pearl Oyster Bar is a small, friendly eatery with sixteen seats at a long marble counter and two windowfront tables. Owner/chef Rebecca Charles' signature dish, a gargantuan lobster roll (chunks of fresh lobster moistened with mayonnaise and served on a toasted bun), puts many a Maine lobster shack to shame. Regulars know to check the blackboard specials.

Sarabeth's Restaurant $$ American

423 Amsterdam Ave. at W. 80th St., Upper West Side. 212-496-6280; 1295 Madison Ave. at E. 92nd St., Upper East Side, 212-410-7335. www.sarabeth.com.

Although Sarabeth's serves breakfast, lunch and dinner, it's most popular in the morning hours and for brunch on weekends. Breakfast fare includes porridge, fluffy omelets, muffins, pancakes and waffles. Try the Four Flowers juice—a blend of banana, pineapple, orange and pomegranate. Sarabeth's also sells a selection of its baked goods and preserves.

Virgil's Real Barbecue $$ Barbecue

152 W. 44th St., Midtown. 212-921-9494. www.virgilsbbq.com.

Southern US barbecue in all its variety, from Texas to North Carolina, is the specialty here. If it can be barbecued or smoked, Virgil's has it—beef, pork, chicken, shrimp, ham. The restaurant barbecues with a blend of hickory, oak and fruitwoods. This unpretentious, two-story eatery also serves related regional dishes like chicken-fried steak, fried chicken and fried or grilled catfish, and a good selection of beers.

Azuri Café $ Middle Eastern

465 W. 51st St. (between 9th & 10th Aves.), Midtown. 212-262-2920.

Don't expect to be wined and dined at this Hell's Kitchen hole-in-the-wall. For one thing, it doesn't have a liquor license, and for another, atmosphere is pretty much nonexistent. But for fresh, savory Middle Eastern food, including some of the best falafel, tabouli and baba ghanoush you'll find in New York, Azuri can't be beat. Trust the chef; he can be surly with nit-pickers.

Dim Sum Go Go $ Chinese

5 E. Broadway (Chatham Square), Chinatown. 212-732-0797.

Don't let the Chinese take-out name throw you. This sleek restaurant, owned by a French food writer and her architect husband, is more sophisticated than many of its Uptown counterparts. New-wave dim sum is served to order, not on traditional rolling carts. Mushroom and pickled-vegetable dumplings, duck skin and crabmeat wrapped in spinach dough, or chive and shrimp dumplings in a ginger-vinegar dipping sauce are but three of more than forty choices.

Gonzo $ Italian

140 W. 13th St. (between Sixth & Seventh Aves.), Greenwich Village. 212-645-4606.

Chef/owner Vincent Scotto is responsible for introducing the grilled pizza craze that is sweeping New York. Gonzo's paper-thin pies are char-grilled, not oven-baked, and use bel paese and romano cheeses in place of the traditional mozzarella. Staples like the classic Margherita pizza, made with fresh tomatoes and basil, are a sure bet, but toppings like corn and mashed potatoes, cumin-scented ricotta, spicy eggplant purée, even watermelon with prosciutto and arugula, are treats that you won't soon forget.

Hale and Hearty Soups $ American

49 W. 42nd St. (between Fifth & Sixth Aves.), 212-575-9090; 22 E. 47th St. (between Fifth & Madison Aves.), 212-557-1900; 55 W. 56th St. (between 5th & 6th Aves.), 212-245-9200.

Fresh, healthy and cheap, Hale and Hearty's soups and salads are a cut above the average Midtown deli fare. Basic soups include Tuscan white bean, split pea, and lentil chili. Specials range from the light and savory (ginger-carrot-artichoke) to the ultra-rich (lobster bisque). If you prefer a salad, pick a bowl of lettuce and let the staff toss you exactly what you want. Crunchy croutons, cucumbers, carrots and red onions are free; other add-ins (hard-boiled eggs, grilled chicken) will cost you. Don't be put off by long lines at lunch; the staff has mastered the art of moving people through quickly.

Jackson Hole $ Burgers

1270 Madison Ave. at 91st St., Upper East Side. 212-427-2820. www.jacksonholeburgers.com.

For your basic American hamburger—weighing in at a hefty 7 ounces—you won't find more choices than at Jackson Hole. Burgers come in 31 versions, depending on the toppings selected, ranging from a Texas Burger (with a fried egg) to the California Burger (lettuce, tomato and mayo). If beef's not to your taste, the restaurant also offers chicken sandwiches in the same varieties.

John's Pizzeria $ Pizza

260 West 44th St. (between Broadway & Eighth Ave.), Midtown. 212-391-7560.

New York has hundreds of pizzerias, but John's takes the quality of the product up a notch by baking them in brick ovens, with thin crusts, a light touch on the cheese, and fresh vegetables and other toppings. Pizzas come in six-slice or eight-slice sizes. With several locations in Manhattan, John's also offers a selection of salads, pastas and sandwiches, and a big calzone for two people. The 44th Street location is in the middle of the Theater District.

The properties listed below were selected for their ambience, location and/or value for money. Prices reflect the average cost for a standard double room for two people (not including applicable taxes). Hotels in New York often offer special discount rates on weekends and off-season. Properties are located in New York City, unless otherwise specified. Quoted rates don't include the city's hotel tax of 13.62%. For a complete listing of hotels mentioned in this guide, see Index.

$$$$$ over $300	$$ $75–$125
$$$$ $200–$300	$ less than $75
$$$ $125–$200	

Luxury

The Plaza $$$$$ 805 rooms

Fifth Ave. at Central Park South, Midtown. 212-759-3000 or 800-759-3000. www.fairmont.com.

This is the grand dame of New York hotels, and has been since it opened in 1907, accommodating many of the world's rich and famous over the decades. Featured in countless movies, The Plaza is a national historic landmark. Guest rooms, all renovated in 1997 and 1998, still have original crystal chandeliers, and many have fireplaces. Almost as well known as the hotel are its restaurants—the Palm Court for tea and the **Oak Room ($$$$)** for dinner—and its Oak Bar and Oyster Bar.

The Ritz-Carlton New York, Central Park $$$$$ 277 rooms

50 Central Park South at Sixth Ave., Midtown. 212-308-9100. www.ritzcarlton.com.

With unrivaled views of Central Park and the city skyline, New York's newest Ritz-Carlton provides the ultimate in luxury and service. Stand-out amenities include complimentary limo service in Midtown; telescopes and birding books in park-view rooms; DVD players and a library of Academy Award-winning films; and complimentary use of Burberry trench coats for guests—even canine ones—when needed. La Prairie Switzerland has opened its first American full-service luxury day spa here, and **Atelier ($$$$)** with its New French cuisine rates as one of the finest restaurants in New York *(jackets required)*.

The Royalton $$$$$ 205 rooms

44 W. 44th St., Midtown. 212-869-4400 or 800-635-9013. www.ianschragerhotels.com.

In contrast to its historic exterior, dating to 1898 (look closely: there's no marquis, awning or even a noticeable sign), the inside of The Royalton is daringly modern. Opened in 1988, it's the first New York product of avant-garde hotelier Ian Schrager and designer Philippe Starck. Sleek, well-appointed guest rooms all have VCRs, CD and cassette players, and refrigerator/minibars. Bathrooms offer slate- and glass-walled showers or five-foot-wide circular tubs. Ultra-hip staffers dress in black.

Waldorf-Astoria Hotel $$$$$ 1,423 rooms

301 Park Ave. (between 49th & 50th Sts.), Midtown. 212-355-3000 or 800-925-3673. www.waldorfastoria.com.

Recently renovated to the tune of $400 million, the regal Art-Deco building reigns over New York City as one of its most classic symbols. Over the years this grande dame has hosted the likes of major world leaders and cultural icons. The elegant, marble-floored lobby reflects the opulence worthy of its history. Well-appointed rooms are individually decorated, and units in the exclusive Waldorf Towers are especially known for their exquisite European furnishings, spaciousness and butler service.

Westin New York at Times Square $$$$$ 863 rooms

270 W. 43 St. at Eighth Ave., Times Square. 212-201-2700 or 800-837-4183. www.westinny.com.

Westin New York is the most dramatically designed hotel to hit New York in a decade. Arquitectonica of Miami designed this attention-grabber: A soaring beam of light curves up the 42nd Street side of the structure at night and appears to pierce the sky. Guest rooms boast sleek furnishings and bold abstract art on muted wall coverings. The health club offers a panoramic view of the city, and "one call does it all" permits guests to dial just one number to have any request fulfilled. **Shula's Steak House ($$$$$)** specializes in serving the "biggest and best" cuts of certified Angus beef.

Must Stay: Hotels

The Algonquin $$$$$ 174 rooms

59 W. 44th St., Midtown. 212-840-6800 or 800-555-8000. www.algonquinhotel.com.

This quiet, elegant hotel is designated a Literary Landmark as the site of Alexander Woollcott's famous Algonquin Round Table. As such, the hotel served as a gathering place in the 1920s for a celebrated clique of writers, including Dorothy Parker, Robert Benchley, Robert Sherwood and others. A thorough refurbishing in 1998 gave all its guest rooms new furnishings and fittings. It has a popular if pricey cabaret, the Oak Room; its Roundtable Restaurant offers a moderately-priced pre-theater menu, and the Blue Bar offers casual dining.

The Avalon $$$$ 100 rooms

16 E. 32nd St. (between Madison & Fifth Aves.), Midtown. 212-299-7000. www.theavalonny.com.

In the shadow of the Empire State Building and a short walk from Macy's, the Avalon opened in 1998 in a building that was totally rebuilt on the inside. Today it's an elegant, luxurious boutique hotel with traditional comforts and modern technology (all suites have high-speed Internet access). Most guest accommodations are suites, averaging more than 450sq ft. **Avalon Bar & Grill ($$$)** serves New American cuisine, and breakfast is included in the room rate.

Iroquois Hotel $$$$ 123 rooms

49 W. 44th St. (between Fifth & Sixth Aves.), Midtown. 212-840-3080. www.iroquoisny.com.

The Iroquois is convenient to Broadway theaters, Radio City Music Hall and Times Square. Bathrooms are outfitted with Italian marble, and robes and linens are by Frette. James Dean, star of *Rebel Without a Cause*, used to bunk here when he was a struggling actor (and rates were much lower!). If you order room service, request a complimentary film of your choice—either made in New York, directed by a New Yorker, or starring a New Yorker to be delivered along with your tray.

Mayflower Hotel on the Park $$$$ 365 rooms

15 Central Park West at 61st St., Upper West Side. 212-265-0060 or 800-223-4164. www.mayflowerhotel.com.

A reasonably priced hotel with a view of Central Park from many of its rooms, the Mayflower is close to Lincoln Center and within walking distance of the Theater District. With more suites than rooms, the hotel offers accommodations equipped with pantries and refrigerators. Guests can get free morning coffee and newspapers in the lobby and apples at the front desk. A small fitness center is available, and the Conservatory Café—also with park views—is open for breakfast, lunch and dinner.

New York Palace $$$$ 896 rooms

455 Madison Ave. (between 50th & 51st Sts.), Midtown. 212-888-7000 or 800-697-2522. www.newyorkpalace.com.

The entrance to this 55-story skyscraper is the 19C Villard House *(see Historic Sites)*, opposite Saint Patrick's Cathedral. Just inside, you'll see the mansion's original molded ceiling before descending the grand staircase into the marble-columned lobby. Oversize guest rooms are decorated with gold-brocade bedspreads. A 7,000sq ft fitness center gives guests good options for exercise. Famed for its award-winning wine list, contemporary French cuisine and elegant décor, **Le Cirque 2000 ($$$$)** is right downstairs.

W New York $$$$ 713 rooms

541 Lexington Ave., Midtown. 212-755-1200. www.whotels.com.

Earth, wind, fire and water are the cardinal elements that inspired this new hotel's Zen-like ambience. Soothing natural light filters through the two-story lobby. Clusters of comfortable couches and a magazine rack make it feel like your best friend's living room. Relaxing earth tones, fluffy featherbeds and top amenities compensate for the small bedrooms.

Moderate

Bentley Hotel $$$ 197 rooms

500 E. 62nd St., Upper East Side. 212-644-6000 or 888-664-6835. www.nychotels.com.

The rooftop restaurant lounge has views of the city, but then so do many rooms in this sleek yet reasonably priced hotel. Rooms have floor-to-ceiling windows, custom-designed contemporary furniture, CD players, on-demand movies, and down comforters. Discounted parking is available. Complimentary continental breakfast is served each morning in the lobby, where there's also a 24-hour espresso bar. Walk to Bloomingdale's and Museum Mile.

Excelsior Hotel $$$ 198 rooms

45 W. 81st St. (between Central Park West & Columbus Ave.), Upper West Side. 212-362-9200. www.excelsiorhotelnewyork.com.

Overlooking the American Museum of Natural History, this newly renovated hotel excels at making guests feel at home. Ask the concierge for help with reservations and tickets. One- and two-bedroom suites come with country-French décor, plush bathrobes and in-room safes. The on-site health club has a good selection of workout machines.

Gramercy Park Hotel $$$ 509 rooms

2 Lexington Ave. (at E. 21st St.), Gramercy Park. 212-475-4320 or 800-221-4083.
www.gramercyparkhotel.com.

The seventy-five-year-old Gramercy is one of New York's most historic hotels. Humphrey Bogart married Helen Mencken in the roof garden; John F. Kennedy lived here with his parents when he was 11; Babe Ruth was kicked out of the famous bar—more than once. Ask the doorman to let you into gated Gramercy Park. Built in 1831, it is the city's only private park and one of its prettiest. Complimentary breakfast is included in the extremely reasonable room rate.

Hotel Belleclaire $$$ 185 rooms

250 W. 77th St. at Broadway, Upper West Side. 212-362-1004 or 877-468-3522.
www.hotelbelleclaire.com.

Built in 1903, this Upper West Side landmark has been home to Mark Twain and Maxim Gorky. Tastefully designed rooms boast goose-down comforters and soothing neutral tones accented by green fabrics on the furnishings and walls. The staff is friendly and helpful, and the brand-new fitness center is free for guests. Walk to Central Park and Lincoln Center, or just stroll the neighborhood—the tree-lined side streets are some of New York's most inviting. For breakfast, get a homemade bagel from nearby Zabar's.

Hotel 41 at Times Square $$$ 47 rooms

206 W. 41st St. (between Seventh & Eighth Aves.), Times Square. 212-703-8600. www.hotel41.com.

Opened in 2002, Hotel 41 is a cozy, reasonably priced boutique hotel that's just steps from "the crossroads of the world." All rooms come with luxurious amenities such as a private safe, bottled water, Belgian linens, down pillows, Frette robes, CD/DVD players, daily newspaper of your choice, and high-speed Internet access. Choose a movie or CD from the lending library and enjoy a drink (either a glass of Chardonnay or a Manhattan) on the house before going out and painting the town red. Well-behaved pets are welcome.

Hotel Chelsea $$$ 250 rooms

222 W. 23rd St., Chelsea. 212-243-3700. www.hotelchelsea.com.

The Chelsea's redbrick Victorian structure, with its wrought-iron balconies, dominates its block on West 23rd Street. Rooms all have private baths and cable TV, but otherwise this is a no-frills hotel with a number of permanent residents. Once home to Thomas Wolfe, Arthur Miller, Dylan Thomas and other literary luminaries, the hotel is listed on the National Register of Historic Places. The old-fashioned lobby's huge wooden fireplace contrasts with the modern art hanging from every wall.

Hotel Pennsylvania $$$ 1,700 rooms

401 Seventh Ave. (between 32nd & 33rd Sts.), Midtown. 212-736-5000 or 800-223-8585. www.hotelpenn.com.

Well-located across the street from Madison Square Garden and Penn Station, and a short walk from the shopping mecca of Herald Square, the Pennsylvania is one of New York's largest hotels. It was recently renovated, as seen in its modern, bustling marble-pillared lobby with mirrored walls. The labyrinthine corridors in its 17 floors of guest rooms can be daunting, but the large number of rooms makes the hotel quite affordable by New York standards. There's a sightseeing and airport-transportation desk in the lobby.

The Hudson $$$ 1,000 rooms

356 W. 58th St. (between Eighth & Ninth Aves.), Midtown. 212-554-6000 or 800-444-4786. www.ianschragerhotels.com.

The stylish Hudson offers a wide array of services and in-room amenities for a reasonable price. The tradeoff—guest rooms are very small even by New York City standards. A short walk north of the Theater District, The Hudson is another Ian Schrager-Philippe Starck collaboration that has drawn attention for its unique and creative public spaces. Its restaurant, the Hudson Cafeteria, features communal tables; the rooftop garden boasts hot tubs; and the glass-floored Hudson Bar overflows with hip young customers.

Le Marquis New York $$$ 123 rooms

12 E. 31st St. (between Fifth & Madison Aves.), Murray Hill. 212-889-6363 or 866-627-7847. www.lemarquisny.com.

In close proximity to the Empire State Building, Madison Square Garden and Penn Station, Le Marquis offers understated elegance at a reasonable price. Black-and-white photographs of New York street scenes decorate the walls of spacious rooms, where the bed is wrapped in Frette linens and the bath is stocked with Aveda products. Other amenities include overnight shoeshine service and a 24-hour fitness center and sauna. Intimate Bar 12:31 serves breakfast, light lunch and evening snacks, and is a favorite with budding models.

The Lucerne $$$ 250 rooms

201 W. 79th St. at Amsterdam Ave., Upper West Side. 212-875-1000 or 800-492-8122. www.newyorkhotel.com.

Occupying a historic landmark property built in 1903, the Lucerne has been transformed into a modern, European-style boutique hotel with spacious guest rooms offering a full slate of amenities, from in-room movies to marble bathrooms and a fitness center. **Nice Matin ($$$)**, featuring French Mediterranean cuisine, opened here in December 2002. Set in the heart of the Upper West Side, The Lucerne is close to the Museum of Natural History.

Manhattan Seaport Suites Hotel $$$ 56 rooms

129 Front St. (between Wall & Pine Sts.), Financial District. 212-742-0003.
www.manhattanseaport.citysearch.com.

South Street Seaport, the Staten Island Ferry, Wall Street, and other Financial District sites are all nearby this small, friendly hotel, which offers rooms as well as suites. All rooms come with complimentary breakfast and newspapers, a full bath, a private safe and a VCR. Studios and one-bedrooms have kitchenettes and sitting rooms; many also feature skylights and hardwood floors. Continental breakfast is served each morning, and coffee, tea and hot chocolate are available 24 hours a day.

Mansfield Hotel $$$ 125 rooms

12 W. 44th St. at Fifth Ave., Midtown. 212-944-6050 or 800-255-5167. www.mansfieldhotel.com.

Surprisingly low rates put this luxury hotel within reach of even budget-conscious travelers. Complimentary espresso and cappuccino are available 24 hours a day. Rooms come with high-speed Internet access, down comforters and pillows, Belgian linens, plush towels and robes, VCR and CD players (music and films available free of charge). Sleek M Bar on the ground floor draws an upscale after-work crowd and offers live jazz on Wednesdays and Thursdays. You can order appetizers here at night and breakfast in the morning.

Washington Square Hotel $$$ 170 rooms

103 Waverly Pl., Greenwich Village. 212-777-9515 or 800-222-0418. www.wshotel.com.

Across Washington Square Park in Greenwich Village, this intimate 1902 property is introduced by the small, green-and-white marble lobby, with hand-painted tile murals of wildflowers. Most rooms have been updated with a minimalist décor of mustard-colored walls and ebonized-wood night stands. **North Square ($$$)** restaurant *(lower level)* is a secret neighborhood find.

Wolcott Hotel $$$ 165 rooms

4 W. 31st St. at Fifth Ave., Garment District. 212-268-2900. www.wolcott.com.

Just three blocks from the Empire State Building, this 1904 hotel offers elegance at a terrific price. Rooms are relatively large and well-furnished, with air-conditioning, safes, WebTV, Internet access and Nintendo games. Free coffee and muffins are served every morning in the lobby, a soaring space with elaborately carved moldings and crystal chandeliers.

Budget

Amsterdam Inn $$ 25 rooms
340 Amsterdam Ave. at 76th St., Upper West Side. 212-579-7500. www.amsterdaminn.com.

For a decent place to sleep at a bargain price, try the Amsterdam Inn. A residential building converted to hotel use in 1999, the inn has some rooms with shared baths, some with private facilities. All have color TV, air conditioning, phones and maid service. Be prepared to carry your luggage up a few flights of stairs—there's no elevator. It's a short walk to the Museum of Natural History and Central Park, and a short subway or bus ride to Midtown.

Cosmopolitan Hotel $$ 115 rooms
95 West Broadway at Chambers St., TriBeCa. 212-566-1900. www.cosmohotel.com.

The longest continuously operated hotel in New York City, dating back to 1850, the Cosmopolitan is located in the heart of TriBeCa within walking distance of Ground Zero, the World Financial Center, Wall Street, SoHo and Chinatown. You can overlook the tiny bathrooms in favor of the location; there are over 40 restaurants within a five-block radius.

Gershwin Hotel $$ 150 rooms
7 E. 27th St. (between Madison & Fifth Ave.), Flatiron District. 212-545-8000. www.gershwinhotel.com.

Young international travelers are drawn to this funky little hotel in the Flatiron District. Though the building dates back 100 years, the lobby's décor recalls Andy Warhol and his Pop Art brethren; on Friday nights the space is turned into a piano lounge. It's a five-minute walk to the Empire State Building. For the budget-conscious, there are a few dorm-style rooms with shared baths.

Habitat $$ 350 rooms
30 E. 57th St. at Lexington Ave., Midtown. 212-753-8841 or 800-497-6028. www.stayinnny.com.

This stylish budget hotel is one of three New York properties owned by the Citylife Hotel Group. Rooms are decorated in earth tones; many have shared baths. Penthouse studios here go for the price of an average room in a Midtown hotel. From here, it's an easy walk to Central Park, 57th Street galleries and Fifth Avenue shopping.

Mayfair New York $$ 78 rooms
242 W. 49th St. (between Broadway & Eighth Ave.), Midtown. 212-586-0300. www.mayfairnewyork.com.

One of the few family-run hotels in Manhattan, the Mayfair is located in the heart of Broadway and Times Square nightlife. Guest rooms and common areas showcase a collection of rare historic photos from the Museum of the City of New York; double-pane windows filter out street noise. Accommodations come with high-speed Internet connections, hair dryers and wall safes.

Pickwick Arms $$ 368 rooms
230 E. 51st. St. (between Second & Third Aves.), Midtown. 212-355-0300 or 800-742-5945.

You can't find a better East Side hotel bargain than the Pickwick. What the accommodations lack in size they make up for by being in an upscale neighborhood convenient to Saint Patrick's Cathedral, Grand Central Station, the United Nations. Most rooms have only showers, and you should bring your own shampoo. Spend some time on the charming rooftop garden.

Index

The following abbreviations may appear in this Index: NHS National Historic Site; NM National Monument; NMem National Memorial; NP National Park; NHP National Historical Park; SP State Park; SHS State Historic Site.

Index

Hotels

Restaurants

Photos Courtesy Of

American Museum of Natural History: 34, 76; Shahar Azran/Apollo Theater: 83; Carlyle Hotel: 92; Cold Spring Harbor Whaling Museum: 107; Cooper-Hewitt Museum: 50; J. Coscia, Jr./Forbes Magazine Collection: 43; R. Corbel/MICHELIN: 24; ©G. Davies/NYC&Co.: 8; ©The Frick Collection, photo: Richard Bryant/Arcaid, London: 37; ©Gioriello/NYC&Co.: 9; ©Group Photos/NYC&Co.: 9; ©Jeff Goldberg/Estro/Whitney Museum of American Art: 8, 49; ©Jeff Greenberg/ NYC&Co.: cover, 6, 9, 23, 27, 29, 30, 32, 41, 42, 56, 58, 59, 64, 66, 68, 77, 78, 79, 84, 85, 91, 98, 103; ©Mick Hales/Metropolitan Museum of Art/NYC&Co.: 36; ©John Hill/ Historic Hudson Valley: 105; Historic Urban Plans: 18; Hotel Belleclaire: 120; ©Brigitta L. House/MICHELIN: front cover (right), back cover, 4, 5, 6, 7, 16-17, 20, 21, 22, 25, 26, 28, 38, 60, 61, 63, 64, 70, 72, 73, 80, 87, 90, 113; Michael Mundy/Ian Schrager Hotels: 121; ©2003 ImageDJ Corp.: 94; Intrepid Sea-Air-Space Museum: 79; Iroquois Hotel: 118; ©2002Kevin Noble/Isamu Noguchi Foundation, Inc.: 101; ©Robert Lipper: 106; Lower Eastside Tenement Museum: 52; Magnet Communications LLC: 108-109; ©Kevin McCormich/NYC&Co.: 7; Metropolitan Museum of Art, Henry G. Marquand Collection: 39; MOMA/ NYC&Co.: 40; Morris-Jumel Mansion: 60; Museum for African Art: 102; ©J.R. Williams/Museum of Arts & Design/Gift of Robert and Gayle Greenhill: 53; Pam Dewey/National Museum of the American Indian: 46; David Schlegel/Neue Galerie Museum: 54; New York Aquarium: 100; New York Palace Hotel: 57, 119; New York Historical Society: 47; ©NYC&Co.: 4, 5, 8, 33, 48, 55, 75, 81, 97, 99; Cynthia Ochterbeck/ MICHELIN: 121; ©Jon Ortner/NYC&Co.: 19; ©Susana Pashko/NYC&Co.: 44; The Plaza Hotel: 116-117; Radio City Entertainment: 82; Rainbow Room: 86; Ritz Carlton Hotel: 95; Paul Warchol/Rockwell Group: 93; San Domenico NY: 110; Sarabeth's: 114; Splendido & Chef David Lee *(Toronto, ON)*: icon pp. 108-115; The Hall Company, NY: 111; Tiffany & Co.: 88; United Nations: 4, 31; Washington Square Hotel: 122; Westin New York at Times Square: 3, 5, 89; ©Weegee/ ICP/Getty Images: 51.

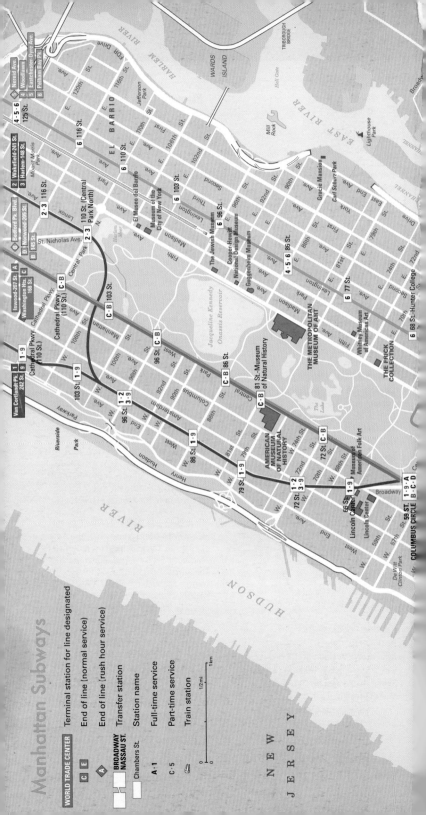